My Next Life as a VILLAINESS: ALL ROUTES LEAD TO DOOM!

VOLUME 5

SATORU YAMAGUCHI
ILLUSTRATIONS BY NAMI HIDAKA

My Next Life as a Villainess: All Routes Lead to Doom! Volume 5
by Satoru Yamaguchi

Translated by Marco Godano
Edited by Aimee Zink
English Cover Design by Kelsey Denton
Manga Lettering by Kimberly Pham

Copyright © 2017 Satoru Yamaguchi
Illustrations by Nami Hidaka

First published in Japan in 2017 by Ichijinsha Inc., Tokyo.
Publication rights for this English edition arranged through Kodansha Ltd., Tokyo.

Find more books like this one at www.j-novel.club!

President and Publisher: Samuel Pinansky
Managing Editor: Aimee Zink

ISBN: 978-1-7183-6664-0
Printed in Korea
First Printing: January 2021
10 9 8 7 6 5 4 3 2 1

Contents

My Next Life as a Villainess:

Jeord Stuart

Third prince of the kingdom, and Katarina's fiancé. Although he looks like a fairy-tale prince with his blonde hair and blue eyes, he secretly harbors a twisted and terrible nature. He once spent his days in boredom, never showing interest in anything, until he met Katarina Claes. His magical element is Fire.

Larna Smith

A very talented woman who holds a high position in the Magical Ministry.

Sora

A young man wielding the Dark Arts, in service to the Ministry. Fond of Katarina.

Raphael Wolt

A young man working at the Magical Ministry. A calm and capable person.

Alexander

A magical tool created by Larna. Physically appears to be a bear-shaped plush toy.

Susanna Randall

The second daughter of Marquess Randall. The first prince's fiancée.

Katarina Claes

The only daughter of Duke Claes. Has slanted eyes and angled features, which she thinks make her look like a villainess. After memories of her past life returned, she transformed from a spoiled noble lady to a problem child. Although she often gets ahead of herself, she is honest and straightforward. She has below-average academic and magical ability. Her magical element is Earth.

Marsha Catley

Daughter of Marquess Catley. One of Jeord's former potential fiancées.

Luigi Claes

Katarina's father, a duke and the head of the Claes family who spoils his daughter.

All Routes Lead to Doom!

Nicol Ascart

The son of Royal Chancellor Ascart. An incredibly beautiful and alluring young man who loves his sister, Sophia, deeply. His magical element is Wind.

Keith Claes

Katarina's adopted brother, taken in by the Claes family due to his magical aptitude. Considerably handsome, and seen by others as a chivalrous ladies' man. His magical element is Earth.

Alan Stuart

Jeord's twin brother, and the fourth prince of the kingdom. Wildly handsome but also surly and arrogant. Often compares himself to his genius brother, and sulks when he realizes he can't catch up. His magical element is Water.

Sophia Ascart

Daughter of Royal Chancellor Ascart, and Nicol's younger sister. Used to face discrimination due to her white hair and red eyes. A calm and peaceful girl.

Maria Campbell

A commoner, but also a rare "Wielder of Light." The original protagonist of *Fortune Lover* who is very hardworking and loves baking.

Mary Hunt

Fourth daughter of Marquess Hunt, and Alan's fiancée. A lovely and charming girl who's well known as the perfect image of a noble lady.

Milidiana Claes

Katarina's mother, and wife of Duke Claes. Has very angled features like her daughter.

Anne Shelley

Katarina's personal maid who has been with her since childhod.

After being confined to the countryside for so long, seeing the capital again, with its beautiful streets and its busy people, filled my heart with joy. As I returned, I was the happiest I had been in the past seven years. However, during the party that my friends had prepared to welcome me back, all of that joy was taken away and replaced with anger.

"How?! How does *that* girl still dare call herself Jeord's fiancée?!" I shouted, slamming my hands on the table and making the tableware on it clatter. "He ought to have gotten rid of that worthless girl years ago!" I could feel the anger heating up my face.

"…That is what we were expecting, too…" muttered one of my friends.

"Then why?! Why are they still engaged?!" I asked her, bringing myself closer.

"We do not know, either… Rumor has it that Jeord himself refuses to cancel the engagement," she replied while cowering ever so slightly.

"Jeord himself?! That cannot be true!" I shouted even louder. "Why would the prince wish for a fiancée like *her*?!"

"That I do not know, but…" she said while retreating even more.

"…But? But what?!"

"Some say that he is adamant about making amends for the scar on her face…"

"The one that is supposedly the original reason for the engagement? I cannot believe that it has not healed after all these years!"

Seven years ago, *that girl* tripped in the castle's garden, and the accident left a scar on her forehead. Jeord, who was accompanying her, took responsibility by choosing her as his fiancée. *Jeord* taking responsibility for *her* clumsiness!

"Knowing her, she is probably hiding the fact that her wound has healed to keep the prince in her clutches. Oh, my poor Jeord!" Just thinking of him being deceived by that harpy made my chest hurt.

Jeord Stuart... the king's third son. The first time I met him, seeing his blue eyes, blonde hair, and handsome face, it was like seeing a prince from a fairy tale. I fell in love with him, and leveraged my father's standing as marquess to have me considered as a potential bride. I would make him *my* prince! I knew that there already were a few other ladies contending for Jeord, but that did not stop me. *I am much more beautiful than them! And smarter! And I have stronger magic! I am the perfect bride for the prince!*

...Or so I thought. Soon after my interest in Jeord was made public, *someone* came to steal my rightful spot as favorite princess candidate. And why? Because of a scar that Jeord wanted to take responsibility for. Unbelievable.

Upon hearing the news, I fell into despair. Had that someone been at least more beautiful, clever, and magically capable than me (which is unlikely, I know), I could have made peace with the fact and resigned my love. But as it turned out, Jeord's fiancée was not particularly good-looking, not particularly intelligent, and not particularly good with magic. Her family's rank was higher than mine, but that was the only subject where she bested me. To think that a girl like *that* would marry the prince…

I had actually met her when I was six or seven years old, as our parents knew each other. She struck me as an egotistical, spoiled, and untalented child. Of course I was not there to witness the scene, but I would wager that she threatened Jeord into taking responsibility for the wound on her stupid face.

I asked my father and friends for help in freeing the prince from his captress… After which, of course, I would marry him. However, as dumb, plain-looking, and inept as she may be, I was still up against a duke's daughter. She would not go down easily.

First of all, I had to make her look bad, and then make myself look good in Jeord's eyes. I started using my father's network of acquaintances to spread the truth about how much of a spoiled brat that girl was. Very soon after that, however, my father got sent off to live in the countryside, far away from the capital… and his whole family, including me, had to go with him. Officially, he had been put in charge of reforming new territories for the kingdom, but it did not take a genius to figure out that he had been forcefully relegated to as remote a location as possible.

He must have displeased someone important… He never told us exactly what he had done, but on the day he received the orders to move, his face seemed to have aged by a good ten years. Also, whereas previously he had always been so kind to me, he was now distant and cold.

Both Mother and I strongly objected to accompanying him, but he would not listen to us, and we ended up having to live in the middle of nowhere near the country's border. So it came to be that eight-year-old me was exiled amongst the cattle and fields for seven years, far enough from the capital that not even rumors would reach me.

Surrounded by nothing but nature, with nothing to entertain me… they were seven years of torture. But I managed to escape this agony of boredom thanks to one of the kingdom's laws. As I have turned fifteen, I am required (or rather, *allowed*) to return to the capital to enroll in the Academy of Magic. There are still a few months before the school year starts, but I insisted upon going there in advance with the excuse of needing time to prepare.

My father — who had remained unchangingly cold towards me since the start of his countryside exile — was not fond of the idea, but I pestered him so much that he begrudgingly gave in, on the one condition that I "lay low and do nothing problematic."

I promised to respect this condition at the time, but that was because I did not know that Jeord was still being controlled by that dreadful girl. Rumors from the capital could not reach me, so I had assumed that my poor, poor prince was now engaged to a different, decent fiancée.

Seven years ago my father's untimely failure ruined my plans, but *this time* I will succeed. I will free Jeord from his engagement… and then, maybe, I will become his new fiancée!

I stood from my chair and made my declaration of war.

"Katarina Claes, your days are numbered! This time, I will seize Jeord from your clutches!"

"Ahh-choo! Ahh-choo! Hmm… Did I catch a cold? Not surprising in this weather… Anne, could you get me a hot drink?" I asked my maid while sniffling.

"Of course," she said in her usual deferential tone before preparing my tea. "However, if I may say so, such sneezes are unbefitting of a lady such as yourself."

"Yep, I'll keep that in mind."

Unbefitting sneezes? How do ladies sneeze? Am I supposed to raise my pinky while covering my mouth? Uhm... Maybe that will work.

Anne brought me the tea, along with some delicious-looking cookies. She really knows how to please me. I thanked her and started sipping my tea, which warmed me up from the inside. Now that fall was starting to turn into winter, even my room had started to get chilly.

Once winter is over, I'll have to enter the academy to study and live there for two years. There's a lot to take care of before moving out of the house for so long! In particular, in my case, I have to worry about the many Catastrophic Bad Ends waiting for me at the school.

Then again, time really flies, doesn't it? I was reborn into this world as an eight-year-old, which means that I've been engaged to Jeord for seven years now. I tried to cancel the engagement so that I would have fewer Bad Ends to worry about, but all my efforts were in vain.

My fiancé, Prince Jeord, once revered as a handsome and capable child, had now grown into a handsome and capable youth. If anything, he had become *even more* handsome, as proven by the many girls in love with him. Since he's smart and a powerful magic user in addition to being good-looking, women throughout the kingdom think higher and higher of him every year.

...On the other hand, the opinion that those women have of his fiancée — that is to say, me — gets worse and worse. Oh well, at least the worst I've ever had to contend with are cold stares and the occasional nasty remark. Nobody here would really hurt a duke's daughter… But what about after I enter the academy? Will I still be safe?

Jeord was cold and calculating in the game, only treating the protagonist to fake smiles as she tried to complete his route. But the "real" Jeord is kind to everyone, including me, and can often be seen smiling and laughing. With all the women that have fallen in love with him, I'm sure that the protagonist will be no exception once they meet. But what about Jeord himself? Despite having so many fans, he never talks about any of them in particular.

I wonder what kind of girl he even likes. In the game, he became infatuated with the protagonist because of her unpredictability and positivity. Will the same happen here? If it does, then being engaged to me would be a nuisance, but I would very happily step aside and give Jeord and the protagonist my blessing… Anyway, no matter how much I speculate, the only way to know how things will play out is to wait and see.

I've read enough manga (and novels, since I was reborn) and watched enough anime to know how this usually plays out… The protagonist falls in love with Jeord, she starts seeing me as an obstacle, and Jeord turns against me.

But if he does that, I'll be prepared!

"I'll go to Grandpa Tom and have him help me with my toy snakes!" I declared while standing up from my seat, half a cookie still in my mouth.

"Lady Katarina, I suggest that you stop playing around and focus on preparing for the academy," said Anne.

"Why Anne, my snakes *are* part of my preparations for the academy! I must perfect them before the school year starts!"

"You surely are not planning to bring those ghastly trinkets you made with the gardener to the academy… are you?"

"Of course I am! I need them for defense!"

"…Defense? Defense from what, if I may ask?"

"Defense from *doom!*"

"Again with the nonsense…" said my maid with a sigh, bringing a palm to her face. I left her to her unwarranted anxiety and went to Grandpa Tom, who teaches me how to farm and helps me in preparing my serpentine defense against Jeord.

Today, I shall make my best projectile snake yet! I excitedly started marching towards Grandpa Tom's quarters… Unfortunately, on my very first step, I tripped on the hem of my dress.

"Eeek!"

I somehow managed to put my hands up in front of me to avoid diving face-first, but oh what a terrible way to start a day. This couldn't be a good sign.

Curse this world and its long dresses! Give me back my tracksuits!

For the time being, I rolled up the skirt of the dress to free my legs from the knee down. *Great! Now I can run to my room, change into my work clothes, and then comfortably go to the garden.*

Just as I took my first step, the door in front of me opened and Mother came out of it. Her initial surprised expression quickly changed into one of stern disagreement after looking at my dress. She'd told me many, many times that proper ladies should walk carefully enough that the hem of their dress doesn't flutter about. Forget *fluttering about*, my hem was rolled up all the way above my knees…

I usually try to avoid any *improper* stuff around Mother — I don't want to get scolded — but I got so excited about my snake toys that I completely forgot about her. Mother's face was not exactly the sweetest to begin with, but now it was slowly turning into a devilish mask of rage. *I'd better… get some distance… and run away… very far away…*

She's known me for long enough to realize what I was thinking, and grabbed me by the collar before I could go anywhere.

"Katarina... Come to my room, will you?"

Needless to say, *"Come to my room,"* means *"I am now going to lecture you for hours on end."* There went my plans of building snakes, or actually even reaching the garden at all, for the day. And on top of that, Mother said that she was worried that I'd embarrass her at the academy, and so I'd need to have even more frequent etiquette lessons.

The day of my enrollment in the academy draws nearer, and here I am, unable to prepare for it.

"A ball?"

"Yes. You are going to enter the academy soon, and it would do you good to do so armed with more acquaintances. A dance party would be the perfect occasion," Father told me while we were all dining together. "I have chosen some invitations from the ones we have received, so take a look and decide which one you want to attend."

My first ball had been earlier this year for my fifteenth birthday, and then I went to the one that Jeord and Alan had held for theirs. But that's it...

The reason why I haven't attended any balls since then is that, at the princes' party, while trying out all of the delicious foods and drinks being served, I ended up accidentally drinking alcohol, getting drunk, and passing out. Or so I'm told, because to be honest, my memories from that day are a bit hazy.

Luckily all of this took place in a hidden corner of the dance hall, and my friends took care of me fast enough that news of my... *incident* didn't spread. On the other hand, I was forbidden from attending balls for a while and had to take extra etiquette lessons, courtesy of Mother.

For a while, *"Your manners! Your manners! Your manners!"* seemed to be the only words coming out of Mother's mouth... *Have my manners improved enough that she deemed it okay for me to go to a ball? Am I free from lessons now?*

As it turns out, no and no. She just thought that, as a noble lady, I was expected to attend a few parties before going to the academy. She also said that I won't have as many opportunities to interact with high society during my two years in the academy, since I will have to live on campus.

So she still wasn't satisfied by my manners, despite all of these years of behaving like a proper lady... She must be a real perfectionist. Whatever the reason, I still had to take those lessons with Mother, but at least I could attend a ball.

Tea parties with my friends are nice, but I only get served light, sweet snacks. I don't have anything against those, but at balls you can eat actual meals, and they're all delicious!

With Keith's help, I chose a ball invitation from the ones that Father had received. I was already looking forward to it!

"Why have you chosen *this* one?"

As soon as Jeord came to visit me at home, as he did several times a week, I shared with him my excitement about the prospect of going to a ball after so long. However, he gave me a perplexed look and asked me that question.

"It doesn't really matter to me. This one's just as good as any other! But Keith said I should go to that one, so I agreed."

I knew next to nothing about high society, so I really didn't have any preference. I'm sure that Father had already filtered my options, leaving only the balls where it was least likely that I'd get myself in trouble. But Keith insisted on that one, and I had no reason to refuse.

"Keith… You chose this on purpose, did you not?" asked Jeord with the coldest of stares.

"I have no idea what you are talking about," replied Keith with the warmest of smiles.

"Is there some problem with this ball?" I ask Jeord.

"The ball itself is fine, but, on that day, I must meet some guests from a neighboring country. I cannot miss such an appointment, nor can I have them delay their whole trip."

"I see, I see. And what's the problem with that?"

The royal family sure is busy… even Jeord, who only has to take part in a few of their diplomatic meetings since he's still pretty young. But I'm the one who's supposed to go to the ball, not Jeord, so why would that even matter?

Jeord sighed. "Katarina… This is a ball, meaning that you need an escort. Obviously you would choose your fiancé to escort you."

"Ahh! You're right!" I had almost forgotten that for balls, unlike tea parties, you need an escort! That's what happens when you don't attend any balls for so long. I should've checked whether my fiancé was free before choosing a ball…

"I am sorry… I had completely forgotten that. But I already replied to the invitation… What should I do?" *Oh snap… I already said that I'd go! Can I cancel that?*

"Don't worry, Big Sister. You could choose your fiancé as your escort, but you don't have to. I will do it."

Oh, Keith, here you go again, saving your sister whenever she's in trouble!

"Thank you, Keith!" I said, relieved… But Jeord looked even more troubled than before.

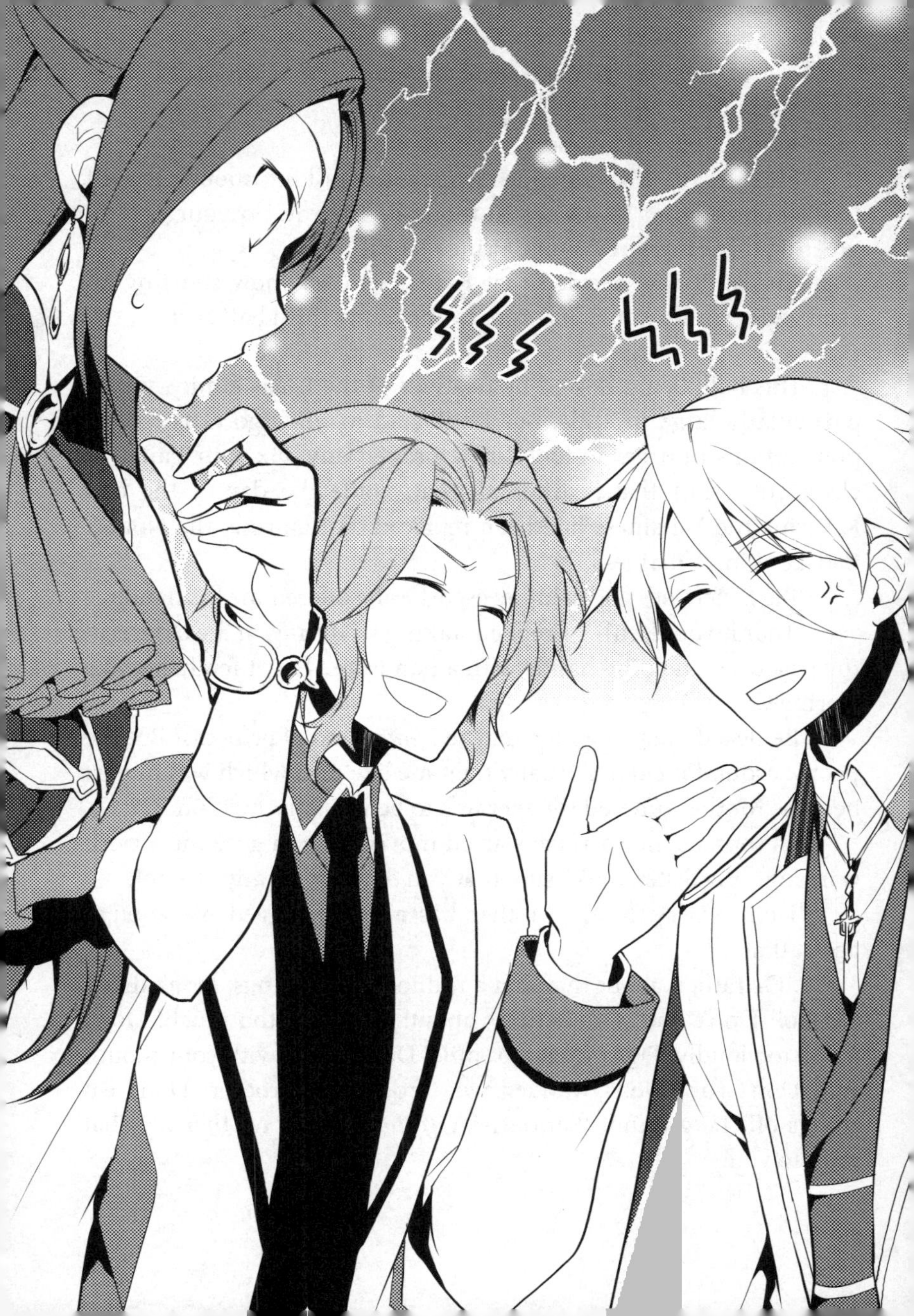

"Keith… How dare you…"

"Hm? Again, I have no idea what you're talking about. Oh well, I will be escorting Big Sister to the ball, but you do your best in greeting those foreign visitors, Prince Jeord!"

And so it was decided that Keith, who was now sporting an even wider smile, would accompany me to my third ball ever.

This ball, being hosted by relatives of the Claes family, wasn't particularly large in scale, but I still had to undergo a battery of preparations in order to look like a proper lady. Fix your hair this, clean your skin that… After all that, come the day of the ball, Katarina the Villainess had been replaced by Katarina, the Not-So-Bad-Looking Villainess.

"Big Sister, let's go," said my escort as he offered me his hand.

"Thank you, Keith," I replied, taking it. Riding in a carriage in my best dress, holding hands with a handsome boy, I really felt like a princess.

Being a duke's daughter, maybe I *am* a kind of princess? But the people around me don't usually treat me like one, which was in part because Mother ordered the servants to be very strict with me.

As soon as the carriage started moving, Keith gave me a stern warning. "Big Sister, make sure that you don't drink any alcohol!"

"Don't worry, Keith. Mother has already nagged me enough about that."

…Or rather, about that and a million other things. Don't drink alcohol! Don't flutter your dress about! Don't eat too much! Don't laugh too loudly! Don't forget to smile! Don't speak with your mouth full! Don't run! Don't wander away from your brother! Don't eat things off the ground! (Seriously? *Off the ground?* Mother… What am I to you?)

"I made a mistake and learned from it! I never make the same mistake twice!" I said, only for Keith to give me a blank stare.

"...Yes, you never make the same mistake *only* twice... I don't think I've ever seen you learn anything from your mistakes..."

"..."

Possibly rude, probably right. I just shut up. Keith kept piling warnings on me, and instead of a princess, I now felt more like a student being scolded by a teacher.

We finally reached our destination, where we met our host.

"Thank you for coming to my ball. Enjoy yourselves!"

After exchanging greetings and some words of gratitude with him, we entered the mansion to join the ball. Now we had to greet all of our acquaintances. Personally I didn't have that many since I'd only been to three balls so far, but Keith had people calling out to him left and right.

Unlike me, he was never forbidden to attend balls, and he often joined Father when he met with other nobles. Still, surely he didn't know *this* many people? He couldn't take a step without an acquaintance greeting him. And most of these "acquaintances" were young girls...

No surprise there, though. He's a duke's heir and he still doesn't have a fiancée. Plus he's handsome and kind to top it off, so of course he'd have a lot of girls after him. I had no problem with that... What I *did* have a problem with was the way all of these girls looked at me.

It turned out that Keith had never escorted a girl to a ball before, so all these girls were suspic... curious about who I was. Explaining to them that I was Keith's sister was enough to stop them from staring at me, but now they were saying that if he was only there with his sister, he might as well escort *them*.

19

Before I knew it, Keith had disappeared into the flock of girls. Mother told me not to leave his side for the whole evening, but she couldn't expect me to go through… that. Anyway, I'm an adult now, and I've also taken all those lessons on manners! What's there to worry about? *I'll just grab a quick snack before going back to Keith. I'm starving!*

I approached the buffet with its impressive selection of dishes. *Balls really are on another level when it comes to food! This meat looks so tender! And the salad! Oh, the seafood!* I was almost drooling.

Where should I start? Go with the meat first, or warm up with something lighter? Hmm… There are so many dishes… I'd really like to try them all out… Okay! No point in keeping the best for last! I'll take that meat!

"Are you Katarina Claes?"

"…Mhfg?" Hearing my name called right after I had taken my first bite, I was surprised and ended up letting out a weird noise in response. I'm sure I looked terribly dumb, since the meat was still in my mouth.

The question had been asked by a beautiful girl of around my age with flaxen hair and green eyes. She looked really surprised when I turned around, which is reasonable since she probably wasn't expecting me to have my mouth full of meat. Then again, I didn't think I knew this girl. She was beautiful enough to be in the same league as Mary and Sophia.

Wait, do I actually know her? I would remember a girl this pretty, I thought to myself while swallowing the meat.

She waited for me to finish eating, and then said, "It is a pleasure to meet you again after all this time. I am Marsha Catley." It was the proper, elegant greeting typical of a noble lady.

Did she just say "meet you again"? Oh no, am I supposed to know her? Um, anyway, I'd better return the greeting…

"Lady Catley, the pleasure is mine," I said with my mouth finally free.

"By the way, Lady Katarina, are you still engaged to Prince Jeord?" asked Marsha, the beautiful girl who I had apparently already met before.

"Oh… Y-Yes, I am," I stuttered, surprised by her question, and Marsha's beautiful face turned red with anger.

"Renounce that engagement forthwith!"

"…Huh?" *Noblewoman speech is always so hard to understand. Renounce the engagement for sweets? What?*

"We only have the main courses here, but I'm sure we'll also get desserts… I don't think that'd be necessary…"

"What are you talking about?!"

What is she mad about? What's going on?

"Look at you, pretending not to understand! Pretense! Lies! This is what your engagement with Jeord is built upon!"

Ohhhh, so it's about Jeord! Jeord was really popular, so I was used to girls hating me for being his fiancée. *"She's not worthy," "She's not fit for a prince"*… I'd heard it all. Well, to be honest, I also agreed with those sentiments.

"Leave the poor prince alone! You have held him in shackles for seven years now! Are you not satisfied?!"

I had never heard someone say such a thing straight to my face. And also, she was basically saying that I had forced Jeord into the engagement…

Her voice was so loud that the people around us, one by one, started noticing.

This is bad. If Mother catches wind of me standing out so much during the ball, she'll probably give me a good scolding... How can I reason with this girl?

"Big Sister? What happened?"

"Keith!" My brother, as always, had come to save me from trouble, followed by a legion of girls. I tried to explain to him that this beautiful girl had just gotten angry at me for something related to Jeord, but she spoke first.

"Are you Keith Claes?" she asked him.

"Indeed. And who are you?"

"I am Marsha Catley. I have heard much about you. Seven years ago you became heir to the Claes family, did you not?"

"Yes, I did... And what of it?"

"You poor soul..." she said, burying her face in her hands.

Huh? What? We just stood there, confused, then Marsha started shouting again.

"What a cruel thing to force upon you! And all because she knew that, being adopted, you were in no position to refuse! And on top of that, to even force you to escort her!" She then looked Keith in the eyes, and tenderly told him, "I shall save you too, Keith! Do not worry!"

Marsha then went back to staring at me and much less tenderly declared "Prepare yourself!" before turning her heels and leaving with an "Until then!" like some sort of movie villain.

Keith and I stared in silence, appalled, until he asked me, "Who in the world was that?"

"I have no idea..." She was probably one of the many girls who hoped to marry Jeord, but she was a bit more... *enthusiastic* than all the others. I thought that she was someone I was supposed to know but had forgotten, but Keith didn't know her either. And she sure had some wild ideas about me.

I wasn't the original Katarina from the game, and I would never force Jeord into becoming my fiancé. And forcing Keith to escort me? How could I ever do that?

It's true that, having been adopted from a distant relative, some could consider Keith as lower-ranking than the rest of the family. But Father had always treated us equally, and Mother... Well, if anything, she liked Keith better...

But I'd never actually asked Keith himself how he felt about that. Whatever I ask of him, he always nods and smiles, be it helping me with the fields, going to the city together, escorting me to the ball... I had never considered it, but maybe he really was doing all of that because he thought that, as an adopted member of the family, he couldn't refuse. Had I forced my poor brother to suffer, being too oblivious to realize his real feelings? Did he actually hate me?! Why had I not realized?! *Ahh, Katarina, you fool!*

"Keith! I'm so sorry! Do you already hate me? I promise I'll be careful from now on!"

I tried to apologize to Keith, but he only got even more confused. "Huh? Why would I hate you? What are you even apologizing for?"

I explained that I was worried I had been asking too much of him and that he only accepted because, being adopted, he couldn't stand up to me.

"Big Sister, once you get a crazy idea in that head of yours there's no stopping you, is there?" he said with a wry laugh, before tapping me gently on the forehead. "I may only be an adopted member of the Claes family, but nobody has ever used that fact against me. I only follow you because I want to. I could never hate you," he continued with a smile.

Phew! He doesn't hate me!

I was so relieved that I forgot that I was in the middle of a ball and hugged him. "Thank you, Keith! My beloved brother!" He would usually scold me for not behaving like a proper lady whenever I did something like this, but for some reason, this time he just stood there, motionless…

Our hug was long enough that it became the subject of gossip and eventually reached Mother, who jumped at the opportunity to scold me for my *most unladylike behavior.*

Father later told me that I had met Marsha the year before I got engaged to Jeord. "It was just once, and a long time ago at that! I'm not surprised you forgot it," said Father, laughing.

I had to admit that he was right. I had forgotten her, and, knowing myself, I'd probably forget about her again in just a few days…

My name is Marsha Catley, and my mission is to free my beautiful Prince Jeord from the clutches of Katarina Claes.

When my father was stripped of his power and forced to live in the country, I lost all of my useful connections as well as access to the capital. I could no longer follow my plan to force Katarina to renounce the engagement by spreading word of her wrongdoings.

I had to come up with something else. She was the daughter of a duke, placing her above me in the hierarchy of noble society. Complaining that she was not fit to be a princess would hardly do anything.

Unable to formulate a new plan on my own, I sought out other young noble ladies who, like me, used to be bride candidates for Jeord.

They were able to provide me with information about Katarina. It turned out that she had not changed much in these seven years, and she still was not particularly beautiful, intelligent, or versed in magic.

All the other ladies shared my indignation in seeing such an undeserving girl engaged to the prince. But as soon as I suggested that we band together to take down Katarina, their expressions of anger turned into ones of defeat.

"We should just give up," said one of them.

Was Katarina threatening them into submission? Unforgivable!

Now armed with even more anger, but still no plan, I decided that my best option would be to confront her directly. I needed to see for myself what kind of harpy she had grown into over the past seven years.

With the help of one of my old connections, I found out about a ball that Katarina was going to attend — and made sure to go there myself.

It was a rather large ball in a rather large manor. It was nothing out of the ordinary, but there were a fair number of young ladies in attendance.

I was not so sure that I could recognize the grown-up Katarina amongst them. I had almost completely forgotten her face. But one face that I could never forget was that of the handsome Prince Jeord, so I thought that I could just look for him, since he would certainly be escorting his fiancée.

And, of course, I was also looking forward to seeing Jeord himself after all these years… which made it all the more shocking when I could not find him at the ball.

I started fearing that my connection had given me some unreliable information, and that Katarina was not actually attending this ball. I asked some of the other attendees and found out that while Katarina was indeed present, Jeord could not make it because of some official affairs, and her adopted brother was escorting her instead.

Poor Jeord, who could not stand Katarina's company any longer, surely made something up to avoid escorting her to the ball... And I also feel bad for Keith Claes, who is forced to act as substitute for the prince.

I had heard that since the duke's only child had been engaged to the prince, he had adopted Keith from a low-ranking branch of the family to succeed him. Katarina was probably bossing her brother around by leveraging her position as the duke's natural child.

Forcing a helpless boy to escort her... What a monster. Unforgivable!

But oh, she will hear from me. Very soon.

I asked around to find Katarina, and I was directed to a brown-haired girl standing alone in a corner of the hall. I walked up to that corner, and, standing behind her, I gathered my breath and finally confronted her.

"Are you Katarina Claes?"

This was the first time I had seen her in seven years... *Wait, what is this?* I was so shocked that I froze. The girl who turned around to reply had the familiar sharp eyes of a villainess... but what caught my attention was how she had something... in her mouth.

Katarina, still chewing, stared at me with a dumbfounded expression. I waited, confused, while she finished eating.

What is going on? Did the rules of etiquette change while I was away from the capital? Why is she still eating nonchalantly? Am I just hallucinating, tired from attending my first ball in such a long time?

...Finally, she finished eating and I came out of my trance. She smiled at me inquisitively. *That just now was nothing but a hallucination. I am positive. I shall just forget about it.*

I was the one to call out to her first, so I had to at least greet her properly. "It is a pleasure to see you again after all this time. I am Marsha Catley."

"Lady Catley, the pleasure is mine," she replied. It seemed that she had at least learned how to greet her peers like a lady. I wasted no time and asked her whether she was still engaged to Jeord.

"Oh... Y-Yes, I am," she replied with a nod.

I could not contain my anger at how impudent her matter-of-fact reply sounded.

"Renounce that engagement forthwith!" I screamed at her, raising my voice more than I had intended to. When I thought about my poor Jeord, the pain was so unbearable that I could not stay collected.

Unconcerned, she just muttered some nonsense about desserts.

What a detestable girl, I thought, becoming even more angry.

"Look at you, pretending not to understand! Pretense! Lies! This is what your engagement with Jeord is built upon!"

She had been using a tiny scar to maintain an engagement that, with her less than excellent qualities, she could normally only dream of.

"Leave the poor prince alone! You have held him in shackles for seven years now! Are you not satisfied?!" Angered beyond my predictions, I kept shouting in Katarina's face.

She just looked at me in silence, unruffled. She probably thought that someone of lower rank than her was not worth arguing with. After all these years, she was still just as arrogant!

As I bit my lip in anger, we were approached by a young man.

"Big Sister? What happened?"

"Keith!" Katarina greeted him.

I realized that this could be the rumored brother, and he confirmed it as I asked him whether he actually was Keith Claes.

He was very handsome, but his flaxen hair and blue eyes gave off a different, more sensual impression than that of Prince Jeord.

"I am Marsha Catley. I have heard much about you. Seven years ago you became heir to the Claes family, did you not?"

"Yes, I did… And what of it?"

Yet another victim of Katarina… She must not be forgiven!

"What a cruel thing to force upon you! And all because she knew that, being adopted, you were in no position to refuse! And on top of that, to even force you to escort her!" I looked him in the eyes, then added, "I shall save you too, Keith! Do not worry!"

I looked at Katarina once more, and, with my chest throbbing but my will unfaltering, I gave her my final warning before leaving the hall.

"Prepare yourself!"

I always did my best to avoid interacting with him, but this time I just had to tell him. After all, if she went to another ball, he would likely be the one to escort her… unfortunately.

I was planning on sending a letter, but since Father had to go to the castle for his own reasons, I decided to go with him and meet Jeord in person.

When I reluctantly entered his room, the prince greeted me with a smile. "Keith, rare for you to come visit me."

His smile was unnatural; his mouth was curled but his eyes looked cold and unwelcoming. However, I was probably the only one to notice that his smile was fake. His servants waiting inside the room seemed none the wiser, but that was because they had never seen Jeord's real smile, the one he only ever showed, as far as I knew, in the presence of Katarina.

Katarina must have been special to him, which was why he strived for her as he did.

But she was also special to me, and I did not want anyone else to have her. This meant that Jeord and I were not friends, but rivals. Today, too, I was planning to leave as soon as I had told him about the ball.

"Jeord, there is something you should know about the ball the other day."

Jeord's handsome brow lowered the slightest bit. "Oh, the one where you took advantage of my official duties to escort Katarina? That ball?" he said with a malicious smile. He was still upset about it…

"Yes, that would be the one," I replied.

You are always escorting her as her fiancé, is it that much of an issue if I get to do it just once? That was what I was actually thinking, but I did not want things to escalate. Jeord, in spite of his elegant, prince-like demeanor, actually had a very dark personality.

"A girl at the ball was berating Big Sister."

"Berating? As they always do?"

Indeed, young ladies who used to be potential fiancées for Jeord never missed an opportunity to scorn Katarina. But they would do so between themselves, just loudly enough that she could hear them, without ever addressing her directly.

A normal girl, if she were the target of such harassment, would probably fall into gloom and stay there for a while, but Big Sister...

"The ladies at this ball weren't very creative with their insults. They just used the usual 'inelegant' and 'plain,' but nothing original. It was so boring!" she said. By the next day, she seemed to have forgotten about it completely. Their insults just bounced off of her...

I never seriously considered putting a stop to this harassment. There were too many perpetrators to deal with them all, their words never escalated to anything harmful, and, most importantly, Katarina herself didn't mind them at all. However, this time things looked more dangerous than usual. After all, that girl had basically declared war on Katarina.

I asked Jeord if he knew anything about her.

"Oh, that Marsha Catley?" he said with a bitter laugh.

"Do you know each other?"

Apparently Marsha had met Katarina before she was engaged to Prince Jeord (not that Big Sister remembered any of it), but had he met her too?

"We used to, somewhat. She can use magic, so she is probably back in the capital to enter the academy come spring," said Jeord, before muttering to himself, "I am surprised that her father did not tell her anything, though..."

"What?" I asked him suspiciously.

"Worry not. I shall take care of Marsha myself," he replied with his widest smile so far.

There was something unsettling about his smile, and it made me worry about what would become of that Marsha girl. Well, if she really planned to do my sister any harm, then she would be getting what she deserved.

"But now, Keith, there is something else I would like to ask you about," asked Jeord, now back to his usual fake smile.

"What might that be?"

"I have heard that during the ball you got rather... close with Katarina. I would like to hear the details, if you do not mind."

I stayed silent as his smile sent shivers down my spine.

"Come on, Keith, I am all ears."

And, with that, I had to stay at the castle much longer than I had originally planned.

Mother scolded me for what had happened during the ball, but she didn't forbid me from attending other ones, since my enrollment in the academy was getting closer and closer.

I would actually go to another ball soon, since Jeord had invited me and would be escorting me. Keith, who had escorted me last time, said that he had something to do and couldn't make it. He looked really worried, so it must have been something important.

I'd feel better if he was there at the ball with me, but I just told him that it was too bad he was busy, and to take care.

He then said that *I* should take care, very much so. I assured him that this time I wouldn't do anything that might stand out, but he frowned and said that wasn't what he was talking about.

"Then what is it?" I tried asking him, but he wouldn't tell me. I never found out what he was talking about.

As it turns out, this ball would be bigger than the last one, with more people attending. *If I mess up around this many people...* I could already see myself locked up in Mother's room, or *the lecture room*, as I liked to call it.

"Be careful," said Mother with a creepy smile just as I was ready to leave for the ball. *I'd better be…*

"Let me take your hand, my sweet fiancée," said Jeord without any trace of embarrassment. As expected of a prince from an otome game. If anyone else tried to pull off a line like that, they would be met with cringes.

This would look much better if he was accompanying a beautiful princess instead of a villainess, I thought while entering the ball's venue hand-in-hand with him.

Once we stepped inside the crowded hall, it was time for the greetings. Greetings were always a pain, but they were even worse when being escorted by the prince. Pretty much everyone called out to us, and pretty much all the ladies stared at me sideways… which was par for the course whenever I was in public with Jeord.

At first I tried to stay by Jeord's side and greet people with him… but I soon got tired of it. *I've greeted enough people for today, right? Right.*

I aimed for one of the few moments when no one was greeting us to tell Jeord, "I am a bit tired, so I will be resting for a bit," before quickly getting away from him.

All these years running from Mother had taught me one or two things about swift escapes. I managed to get away, not because I could run faster than Jeord, but because he was stopped by one noble after another trying to greet him.

While feeling sorry for him, I made my way to the only enjoyable part of any ball: the buffet.

"I see, it's desserts in this house…" I said to myself, nodding with my arms crossed in front of the refreshments.

This was my fourth ball, but, considering that one of them was at Claes Manor and one was at the castle, it was only the second time I had attended one at the home of someone unrelated to me. I realized now that the food looked really different at each ball.

My first ball — the one held at my home — had an incredible selection of all kinds of foods. What with the Claes family being so important and it being my high-society debut, the buffet was fit for a king. And of course, the buffet at the actual king's castle was even better. However, last time I found out that the lower-ranking noble families aren't as extravagant in feeding their guests. That being said, they had different varieties of salads, all delicious.

This time, it was the desserts that were the best part of the offerings. Maybe, even if they can't afford to make the whole menu luxurious from start to finish, nobles have some courses that they just can't compromise on. As expected of fancy people.

The hosts gave their best to provide us with these no-compromises delicacies, yet everyone was so busy greeting each other and dancing that the food was almost untouched! What a waste! It was up to me to do right by that buffet. I took a dish and started with the salads.

When I was busy chewing on a piece of fresh, crunchy lettuce covered in delicious dressing, someone called out to me.

"If you like that, you should try the one over here as well."

"Mphh?" I replied with my mouth full of salad. Between my weird reply and the leaf sticking out of my mouth, I must have looked pretty dumb. The other person, probably surprised by said dumb look, stared at me with a confused expression.

I felt like I was having deja vu. That confused expression was familiar — it belonged to a very beautiful girl around my age, with black hair and green eyes... *Who is she?*

I didn't know, so I just kept chewing and swallowed the salad. She waited for me to finish, then smiled and offered me a glass.

"This drink is delicious. Would you care to try it?"

She hadn't introduced herself, so she must have been one of the many people I'd greeted together with Jeord... To be honest, there were so many that I couldn't be sure.

Saying that I forgot her name and asking for it again would've been very rude, so I gave her my "nice-to-meet-you-again" smile and thanked her, accepting the glass.

Inside of it was a light-purple liquid, probably either grape juice or wine. I sniffed at it to make sure that it wasn't wine (Mother and the others told me to stay away from alcohol), and it smelled sweet and delicious, like juice. *No problem then.*

I smiled again at the girl who had offered me the glass and drank its contents, which turned out to be sweet and delicate. *Wow, this really is delicious... I could go for another one.*

"This is delightful! Where can I get more?" I asked the girl, who promptly offered me another glass. *She's so kind!*

"Thank you," I said before starting to drink the second glass.

...Uh? What is this feeling? I've felt it before... Why is everything spinning? What's going on?

Those were my last thoughts as my consciousness started fading away.

Just before I completely lost my senses, I heard a voice. It sounded like my friend, the perfect noble lady who was the star of the ball...

★★★★★

A few weeks had passed since I, Marsha Catley, had confronted Katarina Claes at the ball. Seeing how she had grown into the villainess I expected her to, I became even more determined to punish her.

I considered several options, but in the end, I settled on destroying her reputation, making her lose her position as Jeord's fiancée and, eventually, destroying her position in high society altogether.

Unfortunately, my father's connections were not what they used to be before his countryside exile, and I also had fewer friends willing to collaborate. I had to work on my own to lead Katarina into a failure spectacular enough to ruin her reputation. This was possibly a quite... underhanded way to confront her. But since she was deviously holding Jeord hostage, I would just be fighting fire with fire.

Of all the plans I had concocted, I chose the one that I could most readily execute and started working on it.

First, I would have to find out which ball she was going to and attend it myself.

Second, I would have to make her commit a catastrophic faux pas in front of everyone.

When my father still lived in the capital, he used to employ the services of a certain pharmacist who specialized in... questionable substances. They were not outright forbidden, but they were too dangerous to be available to the public at large. For example, odorless alcohol and a drug that greatly increases the potency of any alcoholic drink.

And those were the two questionable substances which I bought. If I mixed these two things and had Katarina drink them, she should become completely inebriated. Then I would just need to lead her in front of everyone and she would take care of the rest herself, entertaining the crowd with some unacceptable shenanigan.

It was a good plan, but putting it into practice would be hard. Since she already knew my face, and I had openly declared my intentions to her, she was likely to be very cautious around me.

However, I had nobody who could help me, and even if I did, I did not want to risk my plan failing because of them.

I put on a black wig, changed up my makeup, and went to the ball.

I had changed my appearance considerably, but would that be enough? After all, we had met but a few weeks ago. And even if I avoided being recognized, it would not be easy to trick Katarina into drinking the drugs.

Last time she was standing alone near the buffet, which would be ideal for my plan, but that was probably just a coincidence. There was no guarantee that she would be doing the same this time. My plan was unlikely to succeed, but at least it would be an opportunity to test how far I could go.

I joined the ball very early, waiting for my target. Suddenly the crowd became noisy, hinting at Katarina's arrival. Of course it was not her, but her escort commanding such interest from the attendees... Prince Jeord Stuart. Smart, strong, and handsome — perfection made man. Young, old, women, men... everyone revered him.

I also took the opportunity to take a glance at him. There he was, after seven years! My prince, once a handsome boy, now an even more handsome man.

Seeing my love after all this time sent my heart racing. However, next to him was a woman with the sharp eyes and thin lips of a villainess.

Impudent! Detestable! I felt my brow collapse into an expression of hatred and disgust.

While I was intent on staring at Katarina, I noticed that — lucky day! — Jeord was looking at me. I froze in awe, and then he smiled at me.

Oh, my prince! I understand! You smile at me because you have been waiting for me, longing for me! I shall rescue you from that witch, fear not!

As all guests had now arrived, the ball finally began and the attendees started greeting each other. There was no one waiting to greet a lady who had been out of the capital for seven years, though, so I quickly made my way to the buffet to wait for an opportunity to strike.

If only my father had not been relocated to the middle of nowhere. I could be the one standing in the middle of the hall right now, next to Jeord. Being better than her in every single regard, I am sure that I would be the star of the ball!

And yet there I was, hiding in a corner... Thinking about it filled me with anguish.

I saw a brown head of hair move in front of me, and, raising my eyes to take a closer look, I found that it belonged to Katarina. She was quickly approaching the buffet by herself.

I thought that such an opportunity would never present itself twice, but the heavens must have smiled upon me. I took out the drugs that I had brought with me thinking that I would never have a chance to use them. I then poured them into a glass together with some grape juice, and I moved towards her.

"If you like that, you should try the one over here as well."

"Mphh?"

...Wait, what is this? I was so shocked that I froze.

The girl who turned around to reply had something... in her mouth. Specifically, some kind of lettuce.

Katarina, still chewing, stared at me with a dumbfounded expression. I waited, confused, while she finished eating.

What is going on? Did the rules of etiquette change while I was away from the capital? Why is she still eating nonchalantly? Am I just hallucinating?

I get the feeling that… I have already seen this somewhere… and recently, at that… No, that cannot be true… I must just be tired from all of this planning and thinking.

…Finally, she finished eating and I came out of my trance. She smiled at me inquisitively.

That just now was nothing but a hallucination. I am positive. There is no way that the daughter of a duke would be stuffing her face with refreshments like that… I shall just forget about it.

I mustered a smile and handed her the glass. "This drink is delicious. Would you care to try it?" She looked at me, and for a moment I feared that my disguise was not enough after the events of the last ball, and that she had seen through it.

However, she thanked me and took the glass. I was honestly surprised by her obliviousness. Or maybe she found out who I am, and she just wanted to accept the glass to then throw the juice away?

Katarina looked at the glass and sniffed it, obviously trying to discern its contents. *She knows!* I thought to myself, right before she gave me a smile and drank the juice to the last drop.

Victory! I never thought that it could be so easy. It must have been my lucky day. And then she even asked for seconds. She really didn't notice.

I smiled and offered her a second glass, and she thanked me again. As soon as she started drinking, she started swinging from side to side. The drugs had started working.

Now I only needed to bring her amongst the other nobles and watch her make a fool of herself. And if she tried starting something with me, all the better! I would just need to play the victim, and Jeord would no doubt come to my rescue.

I reached for Katarina, trying to lead her towards the center of the hall, but someone beat me to it.

"Katarina, are you alright?"

Helping Katarina to stay upright was a rather good-looking girl with burnt sienna hair, large eyes, and beautiful pink lips. I had never seen her before.

She stared at me as if demanding an explanation. I did not like that arrogant stare, but I could not resist the silent pressure it imposed upon me.

"I-It seems that this lady has drunk too much, and I was just trying to help her..."

"I see. In that case, she must be brought to an empty room to rest. Could you help me, Miss Catley?"

"Wh-Why do you know my name?!" I had never told this girl who I was.

"We met each other a few times at tea parties many years ago."

Tea parties? Years ago? I had no memory of this girl and her intense stare.

Seeing my confusion, she smiled at me and gave her name.

"I am Mary Hunt, fourth daughter of the Hunt family. It is a pleasure meeting you again."

Indeed, I had met the Hunt ladies at various tea parties at their manor. In particular, I had become friends with the oldest one, Lilia.

But... the fourth daughter? Mary?

...Right! That timid, sheepish girl!

I looked at her eyes once again. Her hair and eyes were the same color, and her face was similar to how I remembered it... but she gave off a completely different aura.

I remember her as constantly cowering, trying not to upset people. But the Mary in front of me looked dignified and commanding, a completely different person. Could someone change this much in seven years?

As I was pondering her metamorphosis, she spoke once again. "Now help out an old friend, won't you Marsha? I found an empty room where Lady Katarina can rest. And there is also someone who would like to meet you," she said with a smile.

I felt myself shivering. My instincts told me not to go... but I could not refuse Mary's fierce eyes, and I ended up helping her.

This marked the failure of my plan, and I would have done better to leave the ball and go home that very instant, escaping from a situation I would come to regret. However, I did not know that yet...

During balls, it is customary to provide a few empty rooms for tired guests to rest, fix their dresses and makeup, or even enjoy a clandestine rendezvous.

There are usually a couple such rooms near the hall, or the guest rooms could be used for that purpose... However, Mary Hunt led me and Katarina into a room quite removed from the heart of the ball.

The room was excellently furnished, much more so than one would expect of a normal resting room. Was this prepared in advance for Katarina and Jeord in consideration of their high rank? I had never heard of such a thing, but maybe the customs had evolved in the past seven years.

I was intrigued, but I would not want to ask and risk being labeled a plebeian. I kept silent while helping Mary sit Katarina on the room's gorgeous sofa.

Katarina still had enough energy left in her body to walk on her own feet (with some help), but the alcohol had made her ecstatic, and she kept on talking about food.

"You must try the desserts here! I've only tried the salad so far… That chicken looked so yummy…"

Once on the sofa, she closed her eyes and instantly fell asleep.

I had now done all that I could hope to do. I had told Mary, who apparently was a friend of hers, that Katarina had drank too much. At this point it would be unnatural to say that Katarina had drunkenly harassed me, and, since Mary appeared near her just as she had finished drinking, my lies would not stand up to much scrutiny.

She may have even seen that I gave Katarina the glass… No, that should be fine. After all, I mixed the drugs with grape juice so that it could look like Katarina spontaneously drank too much wine. And, since she drank it to the last drop, there was no incriminating evidence left.

However, there was something distressing about Mary right from the start. I wanted to get away from her…

"I will be on my way, then," I said, trying to leave the room.

"Please wait. As I mentioned earlier, there is someone who would really like to meet you," she said assertively. Her face had the elegant smile of a noblewoman, but her hand gripped my arm with no intention of letting it go.

Realizing that following Mary had been a mistake, I was assailed by fear. I was unable to speak; I merely listened as she continued with that same smile.

"Believe me, I would love to punish you myself for what you have done. Right now I am only following orders, so I will have to abstain from doing so, but consider this a promise… If you ever lay a finger on Katarina again…"

She closed the distance between our faces, and, with a menacing, low voice, said something that made me cower in fear.

"…You will regret it."

Her expression was terrifyingly cold, and her words made it clear that she knew what I had done.

Scared, I tried to free myself from Mary's grip by pulling her hand off my arm. It was then that the door opened and someone entered the room. This entrance was so refined and splendid that, despite my fear, I found myself fascinated.

"Marsha Catley… it has been a while," said Prince Jeord with a beautiful smile.

"Y-Yes!"

Seeing him after all these years made my mind go blank. *He came to see me! My prince! This must be like in the tales I read as a child. He is the dashing prince come to save me from my captivity in the countryside and bring me to the castle with him!*

As I was fantasizing, the prince addressed Mary. "Thank you for bringing Katarina here. I will make sure to repay you properly."

"I need no such thing. I did not do this for you, Prince Jeord, but for Lady Katarina."

"Still, Katarina is my future bride. As her husband, I shall have to thank you for helping her."

Jeord and Mary were completely ignoring me and talking amongst themselves… but they were not quite making sense.

"She may be your fiancée now, but who can tell about the future? Moreover, someone who is not there to help Katarina when she is in distress is not fit to be her husband."

"That, as I have already explained to you, was part of our strategy. Most importantly, why is Katarina in this state? Had I not told you to prevent harm from befalling her?"

"Well… that is… Katarina moved more quickly than I had expected, and I… lost sight of her. I am very sorry. However, I have had people look into the drugs that would be used on her, and they were not particularly dangerous. I believe she will be fine."

"Yes, I too had them researched. She will be fine."

I stared at the two, whose conversation was getting further and further away from what I could hope to understand. There was one thing that caught my attention, however...

"Prince Jeord, I thought that you detested Katarina..."

She forced him into the engagement and kept him under her command, or so I believed. However, judging by his conversation right now, it would seem that he actually had feelings for his fiancée.

"Oh, you were one of *those*?" Jeord replied to my comment, before turning to me with the most stunning smile and speaking once again.

"I talk of my engagement with joy, and I advertise my love for Katarina at every occasion. Yet, for some reason, there are some people who still believe that I despise her. They are quite a nuisance, to be honest."

"So... you are maintaining the engagement... of your own accord?"

And, he... loves... Katarina? But, she...

"But she is neither beautiful, nor talented, nor skilled in magic! She does not excel in anything! Why?!"

Upon hearing my words, Jeord's expression changed into one so cold that he looked like a different person altogether.

"Someone who hears only what they want to hear and sees only what they want to see may fail to understand Katarina's charm. That is a shame, but I do not care. What I do care about, and will not forgive, is harming my Katarina. Did you not hear from your father?"

Being spoken to with a tone more severe than had ever been used on me was terrifying, but I couldn't fail to miss the prince's last remark.

"My... father?"

"So he really did not tell you anything. Or maybe you just did not listen to him," said Jeord with contempt in his eyes. "*You* are the reason why your father was sent to the countryside."

"What?!" *I am the reason? Was it not just the fault of my father and of whatever he had done wrong?* "...What do you mean?"

"Your father was removed from the capital to pay for your crime. The crime of spreading bad rumors about Katarina."

"Because... I spread rumors about her...?"

The timing matched, but I had never thought that the reason could be... And more importantly...

"But who ordered it?"

I could not believe that it had been Katarina herself. *Had it been Duke Claes, who so fervently loves his daughter?*

Jeord interrupted my train of thought by coming closer to me with a smile. "Take a guess," he said with lips curled upwards but eyes that showed no trace of a real smile. I looked into his eyes, and inside them I found endless cold... and the answer to my question.

Jeord ordered it.

"Ah... Ah..." Wordless sounds came out of my mouth.

Jeord, the perfect prince, the ideal prince, the prince of my destiny... All that I believed about him was crumbling.

"And to think that I had warned him that there would be no second time, and to make sure his daughter understood it..."

Indeed, Father had told me to behave myself once in the capital, but... who knew that something like that had happened? Why had he not told me? ...Or maybe he had, and, as Jeord said, I just did not listen...

"So, I will not excuse what you did to Katarina today."

I could see in Jeord's stare that he was utterly serious in his threat, and I started trembling. In front of me was not the prince of my dreams, but a nightmarish devil. I looked around for help, but the woman behind me was staring at me with eyes just as cold.

Nobody was going to help me.

My parents, in bringing me up, had never scolded or punished me in such a way.

"Ah…" Once again, I failed to produce any complete words. I was so scared that my feet felt glued to the floor, and I found myself unable to move.

"Well, well, how shall we punish you then?" said the devil with a sadistic smile, terrifying enough that my face turned white.

Please… someone… save me, I prayed in my heart.

"Jeord, I think you should stop," someone said loudly.

As I looked to the sofa in the corner of the room in surprise, I saw the girl who had been asleep up until now standing up and looking in this direction.

The devil in front of me also looked at the girl with widened eyes. "Katarina, are you already awake?"

"I think you should stop," she said fiercely again, ignoring his question.

Her clear blue eyes stared into mine, as if to tell me that I had suffered enough and that I was free to go. I stopped trembling, and I could move my body again.

I ran away from that room as fast as I could. The devil looked surprised, but thankfully did not chase me.

I kept running to safety, with my heart beating madly. The prince I had loved turned out to be a devil. And that girl, who I had thought to be a devil…

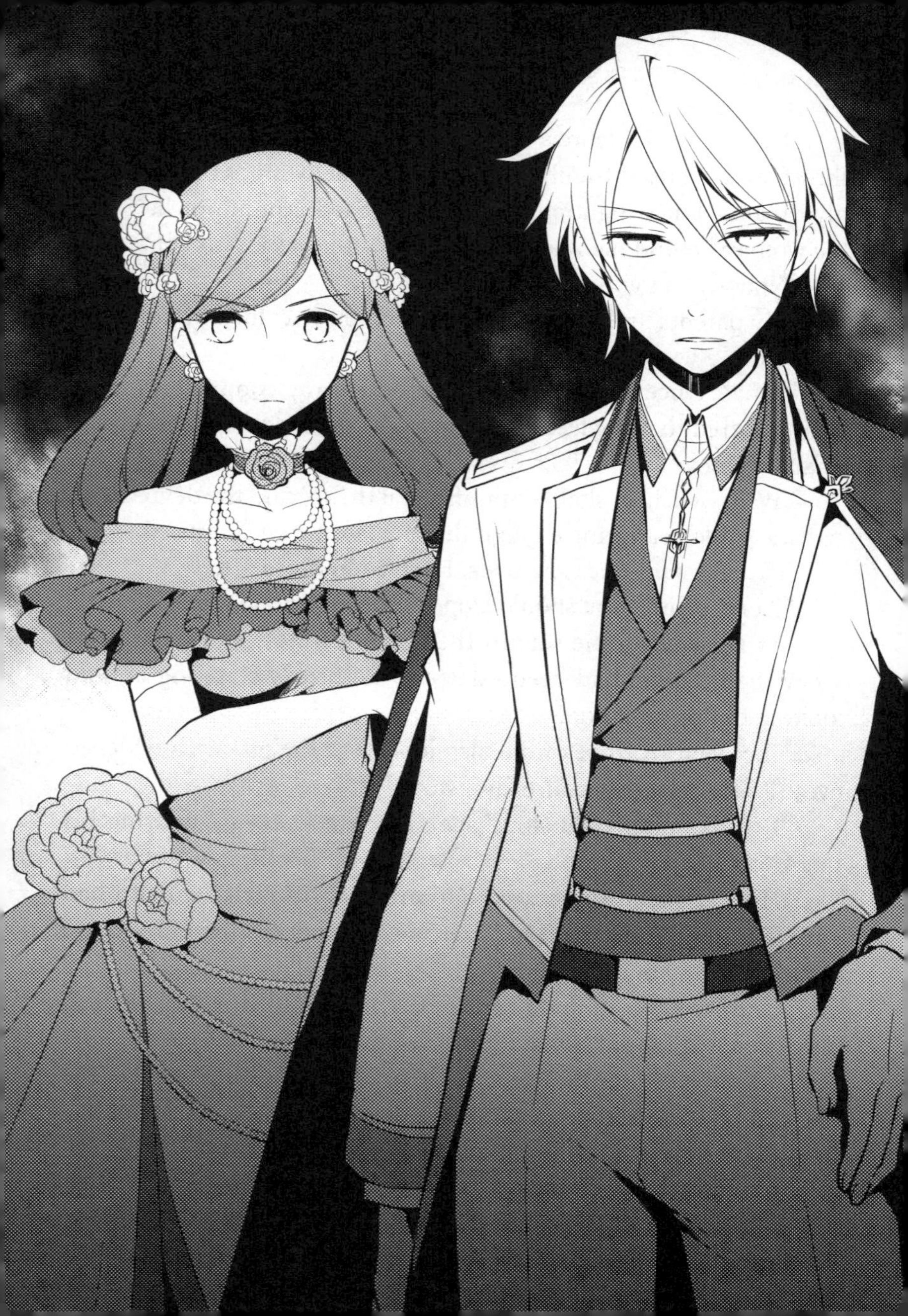

I sighed as I watched the girl run out of the room.

"She ran away," I said, laughing bitterly.

"After how much we scared her, I doubt she will be a nuisance any longer," Mary replied from behind me.

"Yes, I suppose you are right."

After all, the girl had gone completely pale and had been trembling in fear. She would likely never bother Katarina again.

As third crown prince, I, Jeord Stuart, am surrounded by plenty of ladies just like Marsha. Because of my appearance and my skill at playing the part of a good prince, they end up falling in love with an idealized version of me. They think of me as the prince of their dreams, so that is all they see. They cannot nor want to see the real me, which is why, as soon as I show my true colors for just a moment, they become so shocked.

Weary of those ladies, I looked back at the sofa in the corner of the room. My beloved fiancée was sleeping so peacefully and comfortably that I could not contain a genuine smile. She never forces her expectations onto anyone. Her beautiful blue eyes look straight into me, the *real* me.

I do not consider myself to be a good person. If anything, I may be a bad one. But that is who I am, and it does not bother me. However, sometimes, I feel tired of these ladies and their self-centered adulation. The expectations that they have of me can be a burden.

And at times like those, I always long to see Katarina. No matter which side of myself I show her, what she shows in return is always the same innocent smile.

Her smile… looking at it is enough to take the burden off me. I cannot live without her by my side, and I will not allow any person to harm her.

All these foolish ladies chasing after the imaginary, perfect Prince Jeord are sure to be envious of her position as my fiancée. The very moment I announced my engagement, they began vexing her in every way they could.

Of course, I started dealing with these nuisances as soon as possible, but I would get rid of one just to be faced with another. There were so many that I was slowly exhausting myself.

I then noticed that Katarina herself was armored with a skin so thick that even the most ill-intentioned of remarks would simply bounce off of her. From then on, I focused on getting rid of those ladies that could potentially do her actual harm.

Marsha Catley was one of those ladies.

When Katarina became my fiancée, Marsha started spreading ill rumors about her. Thankfully, Marquess Catley had been involved in some questionable affairs, and I was able to use that as an excuse to send his whole family, including Marsha, into de facto exile to the countryside. (Not that I did it myself… I simply provided the right information to the right people.)

Before he left the capital, I also told the marquess that my fiancée should be left alone. Yet apparently that did not make it to his daughter's ears, and the girl started her mischief as soon as she came back.

She had crossed the line for a second time, so minor punishments would no longer be sufficient. With the cooperation of Mary Hunt, whose face Marsha did not know and who would take no issue with my plans, I set up a trap.

Marsha behaved just as expected, and we easily led her into the room we had prepared in advance. I was eager to threaten her enough that she would never bother Katarina again, but...

"I think you should stop," intervened Katarina herself, leaving me speechless. As her clear blue eyes stared into mine, I lost any will to continue. Why did she say that? Why would she stand on the side of someone who had just tried to hurt her? At the time, her words had me so confused that I even forgot to ask her these questions.

Usually, for me, knowing someone for a while is enough to understand their ways and predict their actions. But no matter how many years pass, Katarina still leaves me perplexed. Just when I start believing that I have finally figured her out, there she goes surprising me once again, like today.

How could one ever be bored in the company of such an interesting girl? As long as I have her by my side, no day will ever be dull.

I approached her and caressed her silky brown hair as she slept once again. I could feel Mary's stare stabbing into my back, but I ignored it and whispered softly into my fiancée's ear, so that only she could hear me.

"I love you."

"Lady Katarina. Lady Katarina! Please wake up. We should go back to the mansion."

I woke up to Anne's voice, and, looking around me, recognized a room I'd seen before. "Uhm? Where are we?"

"This room, young miss? Prince Jeord had the host prepare it."

"Prepare it? Jeord? …What does that have to do with me?"

Anne then explained to me that I had lost consciousness during the ball and was brought here by Mary, who happened to be passing by. I remembered absolutely nothing of it. The last thing I did remember was drinking the juice that someone had offered me.

"Wait, was that juice actually wine or something? Maybe my nose was stuffy and I couldn't smell the alcohol!"

"You are not at fault this time, Lady Katarina," said Anne, and then she also reassured me that Mother won't hear about what happened. *Phew.*

I may have lost consciousness, but I felt alright now that I had slept for a bit. Refreshed, even. Now, however, I had to go back home, and I was told that we didn't have time to stop by the main hall.

I was a little surprised that Mary, despite being at the ball, hadn't come to greet me. She usually always rushed to do it… Maybe she came in late? *Oh well, I'll just thank her the next time we meet.*

I told Jeord that I was going back home, and left him alone at the ball. While in the carriage on the way home, I spoke to Anne about the nightmare I had while sleeping on the sofa earlier.

"A nightmare?"

"I had this salad, and I was looking forward to eating it… Then Jeord comes in and starts eating it. I tell him, 'Jeord, I think you should stop,' but he doesn't listen and keeps on eating. I raise my voice and tell him 'I think you should stop' once more and only then he finally stops."

"…What? Did you not say *nightmare*?"

"He was eating all of my salad! And he wouldn't stop! If that's not a nightmare, what is?" I explained to Anne, who silently gave me a blank, inscrutable stare.

We finally reached home, and, for once, Mother didn't scold me! *I did it!*

I had kind of gotten used to balls. Sure, I may not shine like a star like Mary did, but, if I gave my best, I could hope to get to at least lightbulb level.

There was just one thing that seemed a bit off…

"What is the matter, Katarina?" Jeord asked as he approached me, smiling. As soon as he did, that girl disappeared.

I wasn't imagining it, then…

"Lately, whenever I go to a ball's buffet, there's a girl who prepares a tray with all my favorite dishes and brings it to me… but as soon as you come near, she just runs off. Do you have any idea who it could be? She's a really pretty girl."

At first I thought that she could be a fan of Jeord, but if that were the case, she wouldn't run away from him. And if she was one of my rivals, she wouldn't be that kind to me.

"I think I've seen her somewhere…" I said pensively, and Jeord gave me a weird look.

Suddenly, Keith came in and started questioning him. "Jeord, has something happened? That Marsha Catley girl has been staring at Katarina, and now she has started bringing her food! What is going on?"

"Huh?! Keith, you know that girl?"

"Don't tell me you've already forgotten about her!"

It turned out that that girl had introduced herself to me. *What can I do? I've never been great at remembering faces!*

Keith stared at me without saying anything. *I know what you want to say… Forgive me, Keith… I wish I could remember people after greeting them just once, like you two!*

While I was silently apologizing to Keith, I heard Jeord muttering. "I was not expecting this…"

Now that my brother had told me the name of the girl, I made a mental note to call her by name when thanking her next time.

"And now, to the buffet!"

It was finally time to go to my favorite part of any ball.

A few weeks had passed since I had forcefully dragged Keith out of his room, and now he looked at home with us. The magic tutor had finally made it here as well, and we could finally start training. My brother was giving it his best, and I was sure that he'd be able to control his powers in no time.

I also have to do my best and improve my magic! I at least want to be able to use something more powerful than Dirt Bump…

Keith wasn't only skilled in magic, but in studying as well. He had never had a tutor before coming to our house, so he learned all he knew from studying with books by himself. Despite this, far from being behind someone like me, who had always had personal instructors, he was way ahead…

And now, with a tutor by his side, he was progressing even faster. He was perfect even when it came to dancing or etiquette… worthy of his spot amongst *Fortune Lover*'s characters. The problem was that he was so good at anything he did that there was nothing left for me to teach him.

I'd always wanted to have a little brother and be the older sister always looking out for him. The few things I was better than him at were tree climbing, fishing, catching bugs, and other outdoor activities. But even then, he was so talented that I knew that if he put his mind to it, he'd surpass me in an instant… That made me kind of sad.

Isn't there anything that I can do for him as his sister? I really wanted to become a good, reliable sister.

"I see... Closing in physical distance on a daily basis..." I was murmuring to myself while reading the book I had borrowed from the library when Anne interrupted me.

"Young miss, you look captivated by that book. What are you reading?"

"I'm researching how to take care of Keith!"

"Take care of him?"

"I want to be a reliable older sister who Keith can look up to!" I said proudly, but Anne just looked at my book and then back at me, confused.

"I do understand your motivations, but... why *these* books?"

"Well, there weren't any books on taking care of little brothers, so I just went with the closest ones I could find."

"Child-Raising Precepts."

"To Take Care of a Child, Volume 1."

"Animal Caretaking Manual."

After all, I just needed to get the general idea so that I could fill in the details later.

"Young miss... I am afraid those books will not be of much help... Especially the last one..."

"I know, but these were the only ones in the library that were even remotely related!"

I'd been spoiled and pampered as a single child for all my life (at least in this world), so I had no idea how to take care of a younger brother. And in my previous life, my older brothers didn't really take care of me so much as they let me follow them and do whatever I wanted.

I guess one time, when I was climbing trees with them as a kid and ended up falling down and hurting myself, they picked me up like a dead weight and brought me back home. That counts as taking care of someone, right? *If only Keith were a bit lighter...*

"I can't come up with anything good, so for the time being I'm just going to do what it says in these books."

"Try not to... overdo it," said Anne with a worried look in her eyes.

Reading through the books I had borrowed from the library, I found out that "physical intimacy" is important when taking care of a child. *Let's try this out.*

"Good morning, Keith," I said while entering his room, hugging him and patting him on the head. The patting part I got from the animal caretaking book.

Did I do it wrong? He's not reacting at all... He's not even moving...

Worried, I freed Keith from my hug and looked at him... He was standing completely still, his face red. *Oh no! Did I hug him so hard that he couldn't breathe?!*

"I'm sorry, Keith! I couldn't control my strength, and I... I'm so sorry..."

"Young miss!" shouted Anne, who had just barged into the room while I was still apologizing. "I am very sorry, young master," she said with a bow before dragging me out.

I tried to tell her about my plan about physical intimacy, but her stare was so intense that I just caved and followed her to my room, where she then explained to me at length why it is improper for a lady to suddenly hug a man.

"But he's my brother..." I tried to excuse myself, but she said that the same thing applies to family.

"Public intimacy is not well-received in noble society, especially when it surpasses a certain threshold."

Noble society sure is complicated.

"And please… try to think of the young master's feelings."

"Keith's feelings?"

Keith had a very lonely childhood, which meant that he wouldn't be used to receiving any acts of intimacy. That explained why he was so surprised! He just didn't know how he was supposed to react! I just had to get him used to intimacy, little by little. And I should avoid doing it in public! Easy!

"Thank you, Anne! I got it!" I said with a smile which my preoccupied maid did not return.

"Are you sure?"

"As sure as can be!"

Once again, Anne's face maintained the same concerned expression.

So, to recap, I had to introduce Keith to intimacy little by little, and preferably not in public. It was time to make full use of the knowledge from my previous life!

Why didn't I think of this before? This is how we built intimacy in my world!

"Keith, I'm coming in to wash your back!" I said while on my way to the bathroom, with a sponge in my hand and headband on my forehead. Just like I used to do with Grandpa before I was reincarnated!

Unfortunately, one time I had used a rough kitchen sponge instead of a soft bathroom one, and Grandpa, his whole back bleeding, told me to never wash his back again. What a pesky little kid I was!

Learning from my mistakes, this time I brought a sponge meant for human beings, and I was eager to share some intimacy with my little brother.

"Get ready, Keith!" I told him as he stood there, in the middle of undressing, staring at me.

"Big Sister… what are you… talking about?" he said, confused, as I took his hand.

Ugh, of course! He's so clueless about intimacy that he doesn't know that family members wash each other's backs!

"You see, amongst family, it's normal to help each other wash one's back as a form of communication," I tried to explain.

However…

"So that's why today I'll be washing your…"

"That's not normal at all!" shouted Mother, barging into the room with a terrifying expression.

"Mother? What are you doing here…?"

I was so surprised by how suddenly and angrily she had come in that I couldn't say anything else before she started hoarsely scolding me.

"I have heard from Anne about what you have been doing. Explain what it is that you are trying to do here!"

Now that she mentioned her, I noticed Anne standing behind Mother with a sullen expression. I didn't know what she was mad about, but apparently Anne was somehow involved.

"Now that Keith has become my brother, I was just trying to deepen our bonds…" I got the feeling that saying "trying to take care of him" would make Mother even angrier, so I avoided that.

"And what does that have to do with hugging him and bathing with him…?" she asked, her expression now more exhausted than it was angry.

"Mother... are you alright?" I asked her, worried about how dejected she suddenly looked.

She raised her eyes in my direction and started talking, or rather muttering to herself. "This is my fault... I was so preoccupied with my husband that I never took the time to properly discipline her... I am the one to blame."

She then raised her voice and, with determination, said:

"Katarina, I shall teach you how to behave like a proper lady!" before grabbing me by the collar and dragging me to her room.

"Wh-What? What...?" I said, not completely sure of what was happening.

What happened was that Mother kept me locked in her room while giving me a long, long... long lecture on etiquette.

A proper lady shall not hug people left and right.

A proper lady definitely shall not enter the bathroom with a man, even if he's family.

Those were just two of the many rules of proper lady behavior that Mother kept explaining to me almost until dawn. She went on for so long that I got kind of sleepy, and stopped actually listening mid-way through. The next day, I had slept so little that I couldn't even muster the energy to eat seconds at breakfast.

I went to Keith as soon as I woke up, to apologize to him for my improper (according to Mother) behavior. Not only did he forgive me with a smile, but he was even worried about me, since I had been dragged into the room of our very angry mother. *What a kind little brother he is!*

I had lessons and magic training after that, but I was so tired that I could feel my eyelids getting heavier... or rather, as Anne later corrected me, going completely shut.

I somehow managed to get through my duties and went to relax outside, playing and fishing with Keith. Once I sat down under my favorite tree in the garden, it didn't take me long to fall completely asleep.

In my dreams, I was visited by a beautiful vision of an all-you-can-eat dessert buffet, and so I woke up in a good mood. I looked to my side and noticed that Keith had fallen asleep as well.

I was surprised, because when I fell asleep while studying or in our warm garden, Keith would lie next to me, but would never actually sleep.

"Maybe he is tired after everything that happened yesterday," said Anne.

I'm sorry, Keith... I thought while looking at him sleeping peacefully. *He really was handsome enough to take part in an otome game. And those eyelashes! They're probably longer than mine.*

However, as I was lost in his face, his expression started turning darker. His eyes were still closed, but he was knitting his brows and groaning as if in pain. He looked so tormented that I shook him awake.

Keith opened his blue eyes, but they were staring beyond me, into space... It made me worried.

"Keith, are you okay?" I asked, and he immediately came back to himself.

"...Big Sister... I'm fine. I just had a bad dream," he replied with an unconvincing smile.

"A bad dream? You really sounded like you were in pain... I should have woken you up earlier! Sorry, Keith!"

He was fully awake now, but he still looked troubled. I regretted wasting time looking at his face instead of waking him up earlier. *I'm so sorry, Keith...*

"I'm fine, there's nothing to worry about," he said, still smiling at me.

"This won't do. The next time you look like you're having a bad dream, I'll wake you up immediately! Leave it to me!" I replied, wanting to help him in some way.

And then I realized that maybe *this* was what I could do to take care of Keith.

After seeing Keith groan in his sleep, I got worried that maybe that hadn't been an isolated incident. I asked Keith's personal maid to report to me without telling him, and, as I thought, my brother groaned and moaned in his sleep very often.

Never much of a nightmare-haver myself, I hadn't thought about it... but in all his moving from one family to the next, Keith must have been through a lot, at least enough to cause a couple of bad dreams.

I decided to turn this into an opportunity to help him, as a good, reliable older sister would do. When evening came, I made my way to Keith's room, who was surprised to see me barge in.

"If you have a bad dream, I'll be here to wake you up!" I said, taking his hand.

I didn't let go of it until he fell asleep. He was kind of restless at first, but he eventually dozed off.

Unfortunately I also got sleepy and didn't manage to check on Keith all night long... but in the morning, when I asked him about it, he said that he didn't have any nightmares. *That's a relief!*

From that day on, I would sometimes hold Keith's hand or chat with him to cheer him up before sleeping, so that he wouldn't have any bad dreams.

Anne knew about it, but she didn't scold me for it. She even said, "I believe that this is helping him."

I kept on spending my evenings with Keith until he told me that he didn't have trouble sleeping anymore and that I didn't need to keep doing it.

When he said "It's all thanks to you, Big Sister," I was so happy... I had waited so long for those words.

It's just too bad that our roles were reversed soon after that, and I became the one who he had to take care of...

★★★★★

After a few weeks since I took on the name of Keith Claes, I had grown accustomed to it and to life with my new family.

Being able to learn from a tutor was fun and interesting, and I also had a magic instructor who taught me how to control my powers. I needed to do this, so that I wouldn't end up hurting a loved one again. Furthermore, I trained in dance and etiquette as young nobles are expected to.

Katarina, on the other hand, taught me about tree climbing, fishing, catching bugs, and other pastimes that young nobles are definitely not expected to engage in. Every day felt new and exciting.

One morning, Katarina entered my room, as she often did. I assumed that she just wanted to invite me on a walk or to go to the fields with her, as usual. I was wrong.

"Good morning, Keith," she said with a smile, before... hugging me.

Why is she... What?

And then, still hugging me, she started patting my head. That was my first time experiencing something like that, and, what's more, it was by the hand of someone who was special to me.

My mind went blank, and my face red. I stood still, unsure of how to react, until Big Sister started apologizing for some reason.

"I'm sorry, Keith! I couldn't control my strength, and I… I'm so sorry…"

"Young miss!" shouted her maid, Anne, suddenly barging into the room.

All the years of serving Katarina seemed to have taught Anne enough that she instantly understood what was going on just by looking at this weird, one-sided hug. She apologized to me and convinced Katarina, who was muttering excuses, to go back to her room.

Later, asking around, I found out that Big Sister had been attempting to build intimacy between family members. Before coming to Claes Manor, I was never *really* part of a family, which made the whole topic a mystery to me… But I couldn't shake the feeling that Katarina was somewhat misled in her intentions.

Still, as embarrassing as being hugged and patted on the head was… it made me happy.

The next morning I wasn't met with any hugs, and it turned out that it was Anne who had talked my sister out of it. While I liked being hugged, I was relieved that I wouldn't have to worry anymore about blushing to death, and about what I was supposed to do in response.

The day peacefully went on as usual… at least until that evening. I was undressing to take a bath when Katarina appeared with a sponge in her hand and a headband on her forehead.

"Keith, I'm coming in to wash your back!"

This shocked me even harder than yesterday's hug had, and, before I could muster a reply, she started menacingly rolling up her sleeves. Sensing the danger, I instinctively stopped her and requested an explanation.

Katarina started telling me, as if it were the most obvious thing in the world, that bathing together is how families build intimacy. I may not have known much about intimacy or families... but this just sounded wrong.

I kept listening to my sister's dubious musings on what constitutes normal family relationships, when she was interrupted by Mother, who had loudly come to my rescue.

"That's not normal at all!" she said to Katarina, whose confident face had now turned white. Judging from Mother's questioning of her daughter's intent, I'd say that I was right. It didn't just sound wrong. It *was* wrong... and knowing this, I was kind of relieved.

After some more incoherent explanations from Katarina, Mother thankfully removed her from the premises.

"I am sorry for all this trouble. Please enjoy your bath," said Anne, seeing my still confused expression.

She then left and I could finally bathe, but not without frequent nervous glances towards the door.

As for Katarina, she was lectured by Mother until pretty much dawn. Come morning, she tiredly apologized about the previous day. She had been scolded thoroughly, but I personally wasn't angry with her. I was just embarrassed, so I told her not to worry about it.

Sleepy from being talked at all night long, she had little appetite, or so she said. But despite not going in for seconds as usual at breakfast, she made up for it with pastries.

She must have been really sleepy... Later, when she fell asleep during our lesson, instead of waking her up (as I always did) I took a look at the dark circles under her eyes and decided to let her rest.

That helped her regain some of her energy, so that afternoon we went fishing together in the stream by the garden, which is one of her favorite ways to pass the time.

After that, she laid down under a tree (*"the perfect tree for climbing,"* according to her) and dozed off. Tired from fishing and from having spent an almost sleepless night after the shocking events of the previous evening, I found my eyelids getting heavier, and I too fell asleep next to my sister.

And then the nightmare came.

The darkness, the tight spaces, the beatings, the insults... Terrifying memories from my past.

Still hurt and scared, I opened my eyes. I saw Katarina looking over me with a concerned expression.

"Keith, are you okay?" she asked with the sun shining behind her back. Just having her there beside me was enough to ease the fear.

"The next time you look like you're having a bad dream, I'll wake you up immediately! Leave it to me!" she proudly announced once I explained the reason for my groaning.

True to her promise, she started visiting me during the evenings, holding my hand and promising to wake me up should I have another nightmare.

Having a girl that I may have feelings for do this for me felt weird, but it worked. Thanks to her, I think, my bad dreams stopped.

She looked a bit disappointed when I told her that she could stop coming to my room because I could now sleep just fine, but, when I thanked her, her face bloomed with a smile.

...Unfortunately, Katarina's unladylike behavior continued as usual.

Time flies. Before I knew it, seven years had passed since I had taken on the name of Keith Claes.

My sister, slightly older than me, is soon to celebrate her fifteenth birthday. In this country, this is the age that marks the entrance of a noble into high society. The Claes house was busy with the preparations for her birthday party, which would double as the venue for her social debut.

Katarina has really grown up since we first met, but, unfortunately, only on the outside. For better or worse, on the inside she is exactly the same as she used to be seven years ago. One could say that she is still innocent... or still immature.

During tea parties and other public events, she is able to behave as a proper lady. But when she is with relatives or close friends, she immediately loses all restraint.

In particular, she often seems to forget that I, one of her closest relatives, am a man. She doesn't hug me out of the blue or try to bathe with me anymore (I probably have Mother to thank for that), but she still lingers around me in little more than a nightgown, showing a complete lack of modesty... exactly as she did when she was eight years old.

A lot of people are attracted by this innocence: her fiancé Prince Jeord, Prince Alan and his fiancée Mary, the chancellor's son Nicol and his sister Sophia, and the number of her fans grew every year.

Jeord is particularly aggressive in his approach, but Katarina is completely oblivious to his feelings. On the contrary, she has convinced herself that her fiancé is only engaged to her to keep all other noblewomen at bay.

In that sense, Jeord, whose feelings are being ignored, is in the same position as me. That should be a relief, but it worries me all the same. Katarina, never thinking of Jeord as a man, always has her guard down around him. Of course, he takes advantage of that to get intimate with her at every opportunity.

Every day that passes, my hate towards that sly, sordid prince grows fiercer... as does, to be honest, my envy for how nonchalant he can stay while getting close with her.

Katarina always taught me that I should be kind and considerate of women, and I took that to heart. Escorting ladies has never been a problem. If anything, if I may say so myself, I am somewhat popular with girls.

But when it comes to *her*, I just can't approach her as naturally as Jeord does. And actively trying to get... physically... intimate with her...? Impossible.

The reason for this, I believe, lies with Katarina herself. During that most shy of ages, when boys bloom into men, she tried to become close with me and often let her body, growing ripe with womanhood, go uncovered but for the lightest of garments.

Before long, the tension that I felt around Katarina, amplified by the feelings I already had for her, had grown to the point that I withdrew most of my physical interactions with her.

Despite being the closest to her, I am unable to close that small remaining distance. All I can do is look at her and despise Jeord.

Katarina's birthday had finally arrived. To my disappointment, Jeord would be the one to escort her at the party. I had to keep my eyes peeled, lest he make a move on her.

The two of them were dancing, surrounded by me, Mary, and the others who shared my concerns, and the rest of the attendees. *Surely,* we all thought, *he wouldn't try anything improper in front of such a crowd.*

Surely enough, he did.

During their dance, Katarina lost her balance, and Jeord brought her in close to his body so that she wouldn't fall. At least that was what all the others had thought, but I wasn't fooled. He had drawn her in on purpose.

I wanted to jump in and pull them apart, but, difficult as it was, I maintained the restraint befitting the son of a duke. I decided I would at least wait until the song was over.

How long is he going to hug her? Let her go already! I screamed in my head, burning holes into Jeord's back with my eyes... until... he kissed her neck!

That's going too far!

I started running towards Katarina, but before I could reach her, the song was over and it was time to exchange dance partners. Seeing the mocking smile Jeord directed at me while walking away made my face turn red with anger.

And she... she probably had no clue, did she? She hadn't even noticed the mark left on her neck.

"If you would, Big Sister..." I called out to her, and tried to clean it off with my handkerchief.

As expected, she had no idea of what had happened and asked me what I was doing. I didn't want to tell her, of course, nor would I let Jeord do anything like this ever again.

"A small bug landed on your neck, and I was just... cleaning that up for you."

"Oh, really? Thank you, Keith," she said with a nonchalant smile.

Seeing her smile like that, so innocently, took away some of the anger Jeord's deplorable feat had instilled in me. And now, looking at her so closely, I realized just how beautiful she looked today, even more than usual as she was embellished for the party.

"You look so beautiful, Big Sister," I said with a smile, inviting her to dance.

"Thank you, Keith," she accepted.

Dancing was not one of her talents, but she had practiced for this day, and it showed. Being so close to her as we moved through the air, looking at a Katarina who was even more beautiful than usual... I could almost understand why Jeord would do what he did.

She really kept her guard too low, though...

"You know, Big Sister... You really should be a little more aware of the dangers that surround you."

"...Hmm? Aware of... dangers?"

"Yes. Especially when it comes to Prince Jeord," I explained, hoping that she would realize how much he was targeting her.

"Don't worry! I'm all about sensing danger when it comes to Prince Jeord!" she replied, leaving me appalled.

"...Really, Big Sister? To be honest, it doesn't quite come across that way..." I reprimanded her, but she just continued, proud of her supposed danger-awareness.

"Yes, things are perfect! I am absolutely prepared to call off the whole engagement at any time! I even told him just now that I would, and that I would never get in the way of his true love!"

She really has no idea of what I'm talking about. "...How is that... perfect, Big Sister? No... this will not do at all. Did you not see what happened just now? How could you be... saying...?"

Katarina was just so oblivious that I almost felt bad for Jeord and his genuine attempts. "I could even prepare documents, you know? To call off the engagement. And then all I'd have to do is show them to Prince Jeord..." she said, seeing my disconcerted reaction.

"No! No, you mustn't! If you provoke him any further... there may be no telling what he would do..."

What is she even thinking?! First of all, how could she possibly fail to notice advances as heavy-handed as Jeord's? Are we sure that hit to the forehead didn't damage anything important?

For the time being, I just instructed her not to find herself alone with Jeord. She nodded, but I hardly believed that she had understood as well as she said.

Having to look after my sister has made my seven years in the Claes family extremely busy. Busy, but blessed. Here, near Katarina, is where I have found my happiness.

Time in the Academy of Magic went by in a flash. In a few more months, I would become Alan Stuart, academy graduate.

I was spending a relaxing holiday afternoon in the courtyard, thinking back on the memories of my two years here. So much happened in so little time. With highlights like the disappearance during the fall of my first year and the kidnapping during my second year, I'd seen enough trouble for a lifetime.

But what surprised me most was the reaction, or lack thereof, from the center of all this trouble: Katarina. You'd think that after being knocked unconscious by Dark Magic and then kidnapped the next year, you'd end up pretty damn freaked out. But she was so impervious to these misadventures that she barely remembered them. *"Something like that happened? Really?"* was her average response.

Now that I've only got a few months left here, I hope I can enjoy them in peace...

The wind interrupted my thoughts by bringing a delicious smell into the courtyard. *What's that?* It was the first day of the holiday break at the academy, so most students had gone back home, including my brother Jeord and my friends from the student council.

With so few people left, where could the scent be coming from? I guessed that it was some kind of food, but it's not like anyone would be hosting a tea party at the academy during the holiday.

I went to investigate the source of the smell and ended up near a few trees in a corner of the courtyard. Someone was sitting, barricaded by foods in all sorts of containers that were laid atop a large piece of cloth spread onto the ground. I couldn't see the person's face, but it didn't matter. There was only one person amongst all the nobles in the academy who would do something like this...

"Katarina Claes. What're you doing here?"

"Hmfoo?!"

She turned back to face me and let out a nonsensical yell. Surprisingly (yet somehow predictably), her mouth was stuffed with food, and it still was when she first attempted a reply.

"Uoccha ew jooin ear, Pweensh Awam?"

Huh? "I have no clue what you just said. Swallow before trying to speak..."

"Gah, iesh. *Nom nom nom nom...*" She finished chewing and then tried to answer again. "What are you doing here, Prince Alan?"

"That's what *I* was asking *you*."

Katarina said she'd go back home for the holidays like everyone else. So why was she still here? And more importantly, why was she having a picnic in a place like this?

"Aren't you supposed to be home right now?"

"I was... but this morning I decided to sleep a little longer since we don't have lessons anyway, and before I knew it, it was the afternoon."

Typical Katarina... But what about that brother of hers who's always following her around?

"Does that mean that Keith's still here too?"

"No, he went back home first thing in the morning to help Father with his work. I told him that I'd follow him later, but I slept too long..."

That explained why she was still at the academy, but…

"Why're you here all alone? What about your maid?"

"You mean Anne? She went back with Keith to help with the preparations for the wedding of one of our other maids."

"Who prepared this feast, then?"

"The old lady that runs the school kitchen gave it to me! She said that since the dining hall will be closed for the holidays, she wanted to cook all the leftover ingredients so nothing goes to waste. So I asked if I could eat some, and she went to the trouble of packing all of this for me! Isn't she wonderful? But she also said that students don't usually ask to eat any of the pre-vacation leftover meals… Maybe they just don't know about them? It's such a waste either way!" she said with sparkling eyes, holding one of the many food-filled containers in her hands.

It was pretty obvious that at this academy, where virtually all the students were nobles, nobody would go out of their way to ask for food made with leftover ingredients. The exception to that rule, who was sitting right in front of me, was the daughter of a duke — one of the most important people in the country. I was sure that the poor old lady had desperately tried to turn the leftovers into the best-looking dishes she could… and she'd definitely succeeded. Katarina's food didn't look like it was made from scraps at all.

"She cooked all of this for me, and since the weather's good, I thought I'd eat outside!" she said, visibly happy as she cleared all the questions I had about her being there.

I guessed that since she was supposed to leave the academy soon after her brother, there probably wasn't any lunch prepared for her. Hungry, she had then started wandering around, eventually stumbling onto the cooks as they made food from the leftovers. She had asked them for something to eat and they had rushed to plate what little they had in a luxurious enough way for a noble lady.

And there she was, sitting on a large piece of cloth, with all that food around her, enjoying the nice weather in the courtyard.

This girl... I should be used to it by now, but her antics really are... Wait, is that piece of cloth one of those things used to cover flower beds?

Come to think of it, this courtyard was the exact place where Katarina had been attacked with Dark Magic last year. Yet here she was, having a picnic. Despite having been kidnapped recently, she was smiling like a sunflower in May. Just where did she get such nerve?

"Are you practicing the violin?" she said, pointing her ever-carefree gaze at the instrument case in my hand.

"Yeah. The weather's good, so..."

"So you're out enjoying this beautiful afternoon, just like me!"

That was true, but I'd rather not compare my decisions with someone as airheaded as her.

I was supposed to go back to the castle with Jeord that morning. But when I woke up, I saw the clear sky and felt like I wanted to stay here. I didn't hate being at the castle, and I didn't have any problems with my family like I used to. Actually, I was looking forward to learning about royal diplomacy.

But the problem was that ever since I came of age, I'd been involved in the fuss about who was going to succeed my father. It used to be only my two oldest brothers and their supporters who were involved, but lately, Jeord and I had been included too. I personally couldn't care less about becoming king, but the people around me just wouldn't listen.

I couldn't bring myself to waste such a pretty, sunny day dealing with the boring quarrels of nobles and their factions. I wanted to spend it doing something I loved. So I'd decided to stay at the academy and spend the afternoon playing the violin in the courtyard.

Because of this sudden change of plans, I got to see Katarina... I was sure that the folks at the castle would have their complaints, but I was happy I hadn't gone.

"Have you already had lunch, Prince Alan?"

"I haven't, come to think of it."

I had been here in the courtyard for so long that I hadn't even bothered eating. I just thought I'd go back to my room and eat whenever I felt hungry.

"That's perfect! Why don't you join me, then? I've got so much here that I could never manage to eat all of it by myself," she said, showing me one of the containers which was indeed brimming with food.

Nobles normally nibble all the different dishes and, once they're satisfied, just throw away the leftovers. The academy's cooks probably prepared all of this imagining that she would do the same. Little did they know that Katarina Claes, the duke's daughter, always eats everything in front of her to keep it from going to waste...

As for me, I was starting to get a little hungry, so I gladly accepted her invitation.

"This is so delicious! It tastes zippy but rounded, without being too sharp!"

"I have no idea what you mean by that, but I'll agree that it's delicious."

"Try this one too! The crust is crumbly and zingy, and on the inside it's slushy and cushy!"

"What? Well… it does taste good…"

We went on chatting while eating together under the clear blue sky. This lunch was hastily made from leftover ingredients, but enjoying it with Katarina on such a beautiful day made it feel like an exquisite banquet.

"Ahhh, I'm so full! I can't take another bite," she said, flopping down on the cloth after she'd left not a single crumb behind.

Most people in high society wouldn't approve of another noble slouching on the ground like that, but since it was only the two of us, I followed her example and lay down as well.

The afternoon sun was starting to inch westward, but it still shone warmly over the courtyard's well-trimmed grass. Relaxing like that while looking at the sky slowly turning red made me feel at peace.

If I hadn't met Katarina as a child, maybe I wouldn't have been able to enjoy this serene fulfillment. I was happy. Happy… and grateful.

"Ahhh, I can't resist! I don't care anymore!" she shouted all of a sudden, driving away any peace or serenity.

I looked at her, surprised, and saw that she was untying her shoes. Now barefoot, she stepped off of the cloth and onto the courtyard lawn.

"Whoo! Nothing feels better than feeling the grass under my feet!" she said, stretching out her arms in elation. That was a bit too much.

"Do you think that's an appropriate thing for a lady to do?" I reprimanded her. Usually this would be Jeord or Keith's job…

"But nobody's looking! And it really feels good. You should try it yourself!"

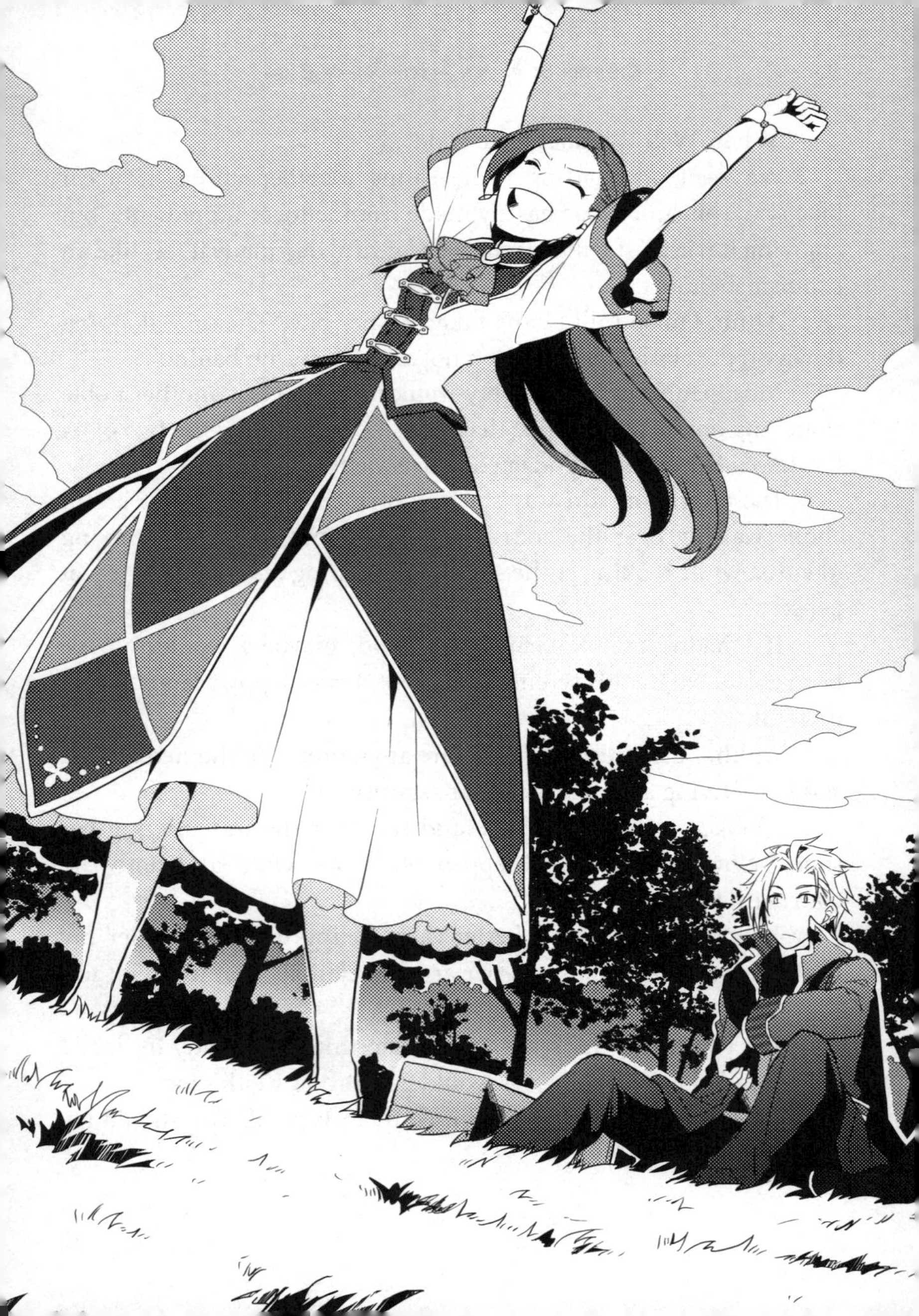

Not only had she completely ignored me, but she even suggested I join her. If I was used to scolding Katarina, like Jeord and Keith were, maybe I could have managed to stop her... but this was a rare thing for me.

And also... she looked so happy with her bare feet on the grass, walking around under the sun... enticingly so. As a prince, I normally wouldn't do anything unbefitting of a noble, but I couldn't resist the temptation of sharing something so unusual, improper even, with Katarina.

I found myself barefoot, stepping onto the grass. It really felt good... I couldn't blame her. I lost myself in the moment and, when I looked to the side, she wasn't there anymore.

She was here seconds ago! What happened?! Did she get kidnapped again?!

"Katarina! Where are you?!" I shouted while frantically looking for her.

"Prince Alan! Over here!" came a casual voice from above.

I looked up and was shocked to find Katarina sitting on a tree branch.

"What are you doing up there?! I thought you were done with tree climbing!"

She'd spent more time atop trees than she did on the ground as a kid, but after her debut in society, the people around her insisted on it strongly enough that she decided to stop playing in trees... or at least, that's what she'd said.

"I've been resisting the temptation all this time! But I was barefoot, and there happened to be a tree next to me, so..."

"So what? This isn't your home! You're at the academy!"

She laughed in response, and all I could do was sigh at this helpless girl.

"Don't worry! Even from up here, there's no one in sight. And the view is fantastic! Why don't you come up too?" she said while playfully gesturing for me to come to her.

Climbing a tree in the academy was absolutely unthinkable. But today — maybe because of Katarina's influence — my self-control wasn't quite working.

I'm already barefoot, and if it's just a little bit... just a couple of branches... were my unusually unrestrained thoughts.

And so, for the first time in eight years, I climbed up a tree. The memory of my climbing competition with Katarina in her garden was embarrassing but nostalgic at the same time. After that (as is the norm for any self-respecting noble), I had never even thought of going up a tree again. Despite this, muscle memory helped me reach the same height as Katarina relatively quickly.

I sat next to her, and she welcomed me with a smile. If we still were kids we probably could have sat on the same branch, but considering how much heavier we were now, I chose another one nearby.

I looked down at the courtyard, which looked nothing like it normally did. It was larger and more beautiful than I thought it was, shiny with its sunlit grass. Back when I first climbed on top of that tree in the Claes garden, I felt exactly the same as I did right now, after all these years. *When you look at it from a new perspective, the world can be so different.*

"Isn't it beautiful?"

"...Yeah, it is," I replied to Katarina.

"I told you!" she boasted with an innocent but prideful smile.

I felt a pounding inside my chest. A year had passed since I'd recognized what my true feelings for her were. I'd probably been in love with her for much longer, but was too dense to realize it.

Even then, with my twin being engaged to her, what could I do? I had to forget about her... which was easier said than done. Her smile was enough to send my heart racing.

"The wind feels so good, too!"

Just there, easily within my grasp, I could see them: her carefree smile, her eyes glowing with happiness. But I couldn't move my arm... I couldn't bring myself to close that last tiny distance keeping us apart.

I was resolved not to tell Katarina about how I felt about her, forcing all romantic feelings out of my mind so that one day in the not-so-distant future I could congratulate her on her marriage to my brother.

I knew painfully well that I couldn't make her mine, but then... why? Why did I find myself hoping that this moment, shared between the two of us, could last forever?

But time is bound to pass and take with it my vain delusions. We couldn't stay on this tree forever. What if someone saw us?

I reluctantly started climbing down, with the intention of helping Katarina's descent once I was on the ground... But I had forgotten about how she was dressed today.

"Wait! Stop!" I shouted at her from below as she started moving towards a lower branch.

I hadn't really thought about it when we were sitting together, but she was wearing a dress. And now, from this angle... I could see right up her skirt.

"I said stop! I can see up your skirt!" I shouted again, unsure if I should focus on decorum or helping Katarina — whose clothes made it hard to move — to the ground.

"Oh, don't worry, I'm wearing trousers underneath," she said, noticing my distress and lifting her skirt.

She was definitely wearing *something* underneath her skirt, but they barely counted as trousers! They were so short that I could clearly see most of her thighs! The view of her bare legs made my face turn red and my heart throb uncontrollably.

I somehow helped Katarina, whose descent was so practiced that she hardly needed any help anyway, down from the tree. Then, still blushing, I shouted at her. "You're not a kid anymore! Learn some decency!"

Her reaction reminded me of a puppy who doesn't understand why it's being scolded, but still looks up at its master. I gave up and sighed.

My oblivious friend and I went back to the dormitory, and thus ended my afternoon of bliss.

The only thing that was left to me after those few hours was the image of her legs burnt into my eyes. A souvenir that would definitely keep me up at night...

As the only son of Count Ascart, after graduating from the Academy of Magic, I, Nicol, had to prepare to succeed my father while helping him with his work. He had taught me most of the important things, and my education as future count was proceeding perfectly... except for one thing.

Despite having reached my eighteenth birthday, I still had no fiancée. This was a problem because I required a wife in order to become the new head of the Ascart family. Most nobles enter their engagements around the time of their social debut, and it was rare for them to wait this long.

It was not that I had trouble finding candidates; there were a considerable number of ladies who would fancy becoming my wife. But the source of the problem was none other than my indecisive self.

My hesitation was rooted in my unrequited feelings for Katarina, friend of my younger sister and fiancée of my childhood friend Prince Jeord.

I first met her when accompanying my sister Sophia to the Claes Manor, where I fell in love with her beautiful eyes and innocent smile. The more time I spent around her, the stronger my feelings became. But I could not make any advances towards her, because she was still the fiancée of my own friend — who actually loved her passionately.

My dear sister had realized how I felt towards Katarina, and, as expected of her, suggested that I make a move. I did not know whether to label Sophia as courageous or reckless. I tried to explain to her why I could do no such thing, but she would rebut my logic on the basis that "stealing love interests is the next big thing." She would then corroborate her theory by recommending a series of books to me, whose titles, always including words such as "stolen love," "betrayal," and "romantic schemes," caused me some concern.

That is why I was still unengaged, bound by a love that I must keep secret.

My parents as well, be it because they had noticed my feelings or because of their leisurely personalities, had not felt the need to pressure me into any matchmaking meeting, as would be the standard for a nobleman of my age.

However, after my social debut and my graduation from the academy, as more and more people began questioning me about my fiancée whenever I was out with Father, he and Mother began feeling anxious over the situation. Among the nobles I had met during official Ascart affairs, some, despite being no older than I, already had a family and even children of their own.

I realized that I could not eternally wallow in my forbidden love and started taking the matter of engagement seriously. I asked Father to make arrangements: I wanted to meet any lady who was suitable to marry into a count's family and who would agree to becoming my wife.

"...Are you sure about this?" asked Father with a vexed expression.

I took this as evidence that my parents did know about my love for Katarina after all. But I had made up my mind.

"Yes. I am sure," I replied with determination.

A few days after I had talked about it with Father, the first few meetings with ladies had already been decided.

"You're so popular that picking out a candidate was the hardest part!"

He said that half-jokingly, but I was relieved in finding that there were still any candidates at all. He found some potential fiancées and arranged the time and date for when we should meet — to my utmost gratitude.

I finally met the first one. A cute, collected girl, who greeted me… and then froze, red-faced.

What am I supposed to do now?

This was not even the first time that something like this had happened. Every once in a while, I would meet someone who would react in that way upon seeing my face. Normally I would borrow the help of one of my friends better versed in conversation than I… but today, I was alone.

I must do something. Why am I such a terribly poor speaker?

I have no issue talking about work or reciting lines in official settings, but chatting in private, and with a girl no less, was completely different and much more difficult. The both of us were standing in silence in front of each other, unable to say anything.

Perhaps I should have had some other acquaintance accompany me today… The servants are still in the room, in a faraway corner where they cannot hear us… but they would never enter our conversation.

My friends, knowing how bad I am at casual chatting, usually took the lead and provided the topics so that we wouldn't fall into silence. Katarina, especially, had the widest array of subject matters. She could turn any trivial matter into something interesting, and just looking at her speaking passionately was enough to make me happy.

If only she were here... I thought for a moment before reprimanding myself. The whole point of these meetings was to forget Katarina and move forward. What was I doing, still thinking of her?

I mustered all of my determination and stared the girl in front of me in the eyes. She blushed even redder and even started trembling ever so slightly. Was she not feeling well? More than once, when she was still a child, Sophia had looked like that because of a fever.

I started worrying about the girl and stood up from my seat to walk closer to her. "Are you alright?"

She nodded in silence, but her face had gone from rosy to pure scarlet. It looked like a fever, and a rather bad one at that. I raised my hand and placed it on her forehead. It wasn't as hot as I had expected, but warm nonetheless.

I realized what I had just done, and— *Curses! I was so worried about her that I neglected my manners. I measured her fever as I would have done to my sister, but touching a lady without permission is inadmissible for a man.*

I apologized at once. "I am very sorry. I should n…"

She interrupted my sentence, not by speaking herself but by loudly falling backwards, bringing her chair with her. This surprised me, but I still somehow managed to catch her in my arms before she reached the ground.

"A-Are you alright?"

Convinced that the girl was not feeling well, I tried to get a better look at her face while still holding onto her.

"…yeee…"

Her weird moan was quickly followed by her losing consciousness and starting to bleed from her nose.

Did the fever get that much worse? I must bring her to the doctor!

I brought the girl into another room so that she could be examined by the doctor, who, luckily, did not find anything wrong with her.

However, when she regained her senses, the girl went back to her home with the speed of someone running away from danger. Before I could make any decision, she had already refused me. Apparently the reason was: *"I can't meet with him again, it's too embarrassing."*

And so ended my first matchmaking meeting, in which I learned just how difficult finding a fiancée could be.

My first matchmaking meeting was less than a success, but I decided that I would do my best in one of the others that Father had already scheduled for me.

The next lady I would meet was a meek, calm-looking girl. She managed an elegant, well-rehearsed greeting without showing signs of blushing or freezing up like the one before her had. She also took the lead in conversation, so that we wouldn't have to endure any awkward silence.

We talked about the ball she had attended a few days ago, about tea parties, and more — or rather, she talked while I nodded and gave an occasional remark, as that was what my speaking skills amounted to, but I felt like the meeting was going well nonetheless.

She was an almost stereotypical noble lady. She had well-groomed hair, fair skin, and the unblemished hands of someone who had never worked a day in her life.

Nothing like Katarina, whose skin had been made quite a few shades darker by working in the fields, and whose hair was often carelessly shoved into a bandana. Handling the hoe had also made her palms tougher than those of the average lady.

And yet, she was so endearing…

No! Stop thinking of her! Concentrate on the girl who's right in front of you!

"And the couple dancing at the ball was so wonderful!" said the girl right in front of me, whose enthusiasm I only half-heartedly returned with, "I see… Wonderful…"

A *normal* lady, during a ball, turned her attention to things like these. Katarina, on the other hand, only had eyes for the buffet and its meats, salads, and desserts. She would describe the dishes with so much passion that one couldn't help wanting to try them out.

…I'm thinking of Katarina again! To no fault of the potential fiancée in front of me, I found myself comparing her to Katarina again and again.

My second trial date was over, and, while it had gone better than the first, my inability to focus on the lady in front of me left me feeling guilty. Despite not receiving an outright refusal of any further meeting, I did not feel particularly motivated to initiate one myself.

Two more ladies came after the first two… but with similar results. I couldn't focus on them as much as I dwelled on the differences they had with Katarina, who monopolized all my thoughts and interest.

While I was torn between the anxiety of having to find a spouse and the dread of withstanding another unfruitful encounter, something happened. Katarina's brother, Keith, went missing.

Always one to leap before she looked, she set off to find him, accompanied by Jeord. My determination to leave that love behind me faltered as I found that the thought of Katarina traveling with her fiancé — *not just the two of them, but still!* — made me uncomfortable.

I was likewise relieved when, coming back successfully from their quest, the two seemed not to be any closer than they had been before departing.

At this rate, will I ever be able to marry?

Dubious as ever, I walked into the fifth and last matchmaking meeting that Father had arranged.

When I entered the room, she was already sitting there, waiting for me.

This surprised me, not only because this had never been the case in the previous four meetings, but also because, as I had heard, men were expected to be the ones waiting for the other party to show up in meetings like these.

But the differences did not end there. The girl who stood up to greet me once I entered the room gave off a strong, resilient impression — a stark contrast with the timid, subdued aura of the ladies I had met so far. If I had to compare her to one of my female acquaintances, I would say that she resembled Mary Hunt.

Right after we exchanged the expected greetings, she followed with a startling line. "Do not worry, Master Ascart. I have no intention of marrying anyone. I only came here because my father insisted I do."

I was baffled by what she said and by the way she said it, wearing the lukewarm smile of someone commenting on the weather. As I froze in shock, she relaxed by sipping the tea that had been prepared for us on the table.

"You said not to worry... I understand that you are not serious about this meeting, but... why would that keep me from worrying?" I finally asked her after the shock subsided.

"But of course, because you too have no intention of marrying, it would seem."

"...Why?" I questioned her abruptly, puzzled by her matter-of-fact words. Did I look uninterested? That couldn't be. After all, I had personally asked for the meetings to be arranged so that I could find a fiancée.

"I have heard from those you met before me. They all said that you did not look excited about the meetings themselves, and that, when they were over, you never asked for a second one."

"..."

I had no idea I had given them that impression... but it makes sense. After all, I spent more time thinking of Katarina than of the girls sitting in front of me.

"Was that not on purpose?" she asked, in response to my apparent confusion.

"...Indeed not. I attended the meetings willingly and eagerly, or at least I told myself as much."

"Women are much more perceptive than you may give them credit for. They would have no trouble telling whether or not you were truly interested."

I see. Women are perceptive enough to see that I still have mixed feelings about this. But if so...

"Will I ever be able to marry at this rate?"

The words burst out of my mouth. I would normally never have let my tongue slip like that in front of someone I had just met... I must have been tired.

As I fell into an awkward silence, she looked at me with a newfound light in her eyes, which suggested a keen interest that had not been there until now.

"What do you mean by that?" she asked.

And so I, persuaded by her look of curiosity, ended up explaining my romantic troubles to someone I had just met. I did not tell her the name of my heroine, but I told her of how I had loved her for years despite her engagement to another man, and of how I am trying to move on and marry someone else, as is expected of me.

Admitting to something like this during a matchmaking meeting would normally be unthinkable, but I had been lamenting it alone, unable to disclose my secret romantic feelings to any of my friends. Maybe I had always waited for someone whom I could tell my story to.

While I spoke, she looked at me with a serious, thoughtful expression until I finished. Then she asked me, "Why would you have to give up?"

Her candid expression and unexpected question made me freeze in place once again, but she did not stop there.

"She is only engaged to another man... What of it? Or do they actually love each other?"

Only...? This girl is truly something.

"...Well, her fiancé does love her passionately."

"But what about her? Does she love him?"

"...I do not think she does, at least for now."

"I see, so your rival's love is unrequited. If so, then where is the problem? Just go and take her from him!"

"..."

It's like hearing my sister talk... Maybe they read the same kind of novels.

"Her fiancé is also a friend of mine, which makes the idea of taking her from him downright abnormal," I said, dejected, as I had to Sophia many times before.

"Stealing love interests is the next big thing!" she would then invariably reply, enthusiastically detailing her crooked ideas based on fiction. All those uncomely romance tales had tainted her poor soul...

But that is not what the girl in front of me did. Instead, she started giggling.

"Abnormal? What would you know about being *normal?* With that face and that seductive demeanor winning you fans left and right, women and men alike... You are just as they say."

Seductive demeanor... Both my sister and my friends often used those words when describing me. They said that I was able to bewitch the people around me to an incredible extent. *"Ridiculously seductive,"* as Sophia put it.

At first I did not believe them. I was convinced that being pursued by complete strangers or even being nearly kidnapped, as had happened to me time and again since I was a child, was the norm.

As I later found out, this was actually abnormal. I had come to terms with that fact... but the girl's "as they say" had made me curious.

"Have you heard about me from someone?"

"Indeed," she replied. "The others in the student council often talk about you, Sophia above all..."

"You are in the student council at the Academy of Magic?!" My loud voice betrayed my surprise at her answer.

"Yes. I am positive that when we exchanged written introductions before our meeting, mine said as much. As expected, you barely read it at all, did you?"

"..."

I had actually read the whole thing, or at least tried to — the worse I felt about this whole engagement charade, the less anything I read would make it into my head. As my reading of the introductions had been less than thorough... I could not blame her for believing that I didn't care about finding a fiancée.

But, if she is a member of the student council... then she must also know Jeord and Katarina. I shouldn't have told her the truth... I considered asking her to keep our conversation secret, but I then realized that this would only make her more suspicious.

While I was busy worrying, she kept on talking leisurely. "After hearing so much about you, I wanted to meet you in person. But Sophia never mentioned that you were looking to be engaged... Did you keep it a secret from her?"

"...Yes."

I did. Had I not, she would have opposed the idea and everything would have become even more troublesome.

"Of course... If she knew it, she would have probably done all in her power to stop you."

Indeed. But how did she know this? "How?"

"Because there is someone that Sophia hopes will become your wife."

My very short question had been enough to prompt the correct answer, but... to think that Sophia was speaking about things like these to other people... I'd hoped that, at least, she had the decency not to disclose the name of that *someone*.

"She is always singing your praises to Katarina Claes!" said the girl with a smile, at which point I felt like passing out onto the table in front of me.

Sophia... do you have any idea of the impact of what you have divulged? And at the academy! Where anyone could hear!

Despairing, I was still thinking of how to scold my foolish sister next time I met her when the girl in front of me offered a word in her favor.

"Sophia admires Katarina so much that she would love to see her married to Nicol," she said, as if to excuse Sophia's advertisement of her single brother as something cute. She was trying to make it sound less embarrassing for me, but hearing a younger girl having to choose her words so as not to hurt me only embarrassed me even further.

If we keep talking about this, she's going to figure out that my love interest is Katarina herself... I have to switch topics.

"Earlier you said that you have no interest in finding a fiancé. Why is that?" I asked, trying to divert her attention in a rather heavy-handed way. After all, I had been talking for so long that I hadn't heard much about her.

And first of all, why didn't she have a fiancé to begin with? She was from a high-ranking family, had magical aptitude, was talented enough to be in the student council. And to top it all off, she was a good-looking girl. She surely must have received a few marriage proposals already... *Is she also in love with someone already engaged?* I thought, but the truth was different.

"I do not want to depend on anyone," she said proudly.

I was surprised, and I didn't understand what that had to do with anything.

"...And that means that you will not marry?"

"Of course! If I married, I would become some noble's wife, and nothing more."

My suspicions were now confirmed. This girl was a bit... unique.

"…And would that be a bad thing? Being a noble's wife?"

"Being a noble's wife and dedicating oneself to one's family and household are very respectable things in themselves. But that would be a life spent in one's home. I want to go out to work!" she said fiercely.

"…Go out to work… like a man?"

"Yes! I have little interest in caring for a household from home. I want to work like a man!"

In recent years, the relative wealth of our country had given women the opportunity to work just as men would. The Magical Ministry, one of the most important organizations in the country, was even actively recruiting women and giving them positions of responsibility. Nevertheless, to nobles, who were extremely conservative in their ways, women were supposed to stay home with their children.

Most aristocratic ladies had but two choices: marry into a man's house, or have a man marry into theirs. This was certainly the case for this young lady, as a girl of so high of a rank working outside her home was almost unheard of.

"But my parents oppose this choice… They are pressuring me to marry as soon as possible, and I know how unrealistic my dream is."

"If you know, then why…?" Society would not look kindly on her for choosing to work like a man.

"There is someone I look up to. She worked hard and now holds an important role in the Ministry. I want to become like her."

A hard-working woman with an important role in the Ministry? I was friends with someone like that, but this person was always tired and complaining about her work… *It must be someone else.*

I removed the thought before the girl in front of me could catch on, and she kept on passionately talking about her idol. "She is not from a particularly high-ranking family, and I had worried that since I am, I could not join the Ministry. But recently I heard that Katarina Claes is going to set a precedent, which gives me hope."

Despite my efforts to change the topic, Katarina's name had come up again... Indeed, it had just been decided that, after graduating from the academy, she would start working in the Ministry.

However, she had a familiar of darkness at her bidding, and a certain superior of my friend had probably insisted that she be hired. Most likely, Katarina's stay at the Ministry was planned to only last until her marriage with Jeord. I had never heard of a married noblewoman holding a job.

"That is true, but I think that there are special motivations behind her being hired, and that it will only be for a limited period of time." I wanted to tell her of these facts so that she would not have unrealistic expectations, which would then hurt her once betrayed.

"I know, but I will not give up. I will do everything I can to succeed," she said without faltering, her eyes flaming with determination. Her expression proved to me how serious she was.

And at the same time, I felt envious of the courage to follow one's ambitions despite what society might think. My ambition, my love — I was trying to sacrifice them for the sake of my household, struggling to find a lady to become engaged to.

The gaze of that brave girl was blinding in its fierceness, but her lips then curled into an allusive smile. "I think that you, too, should not give up. Go to the girl you love and speak your feelings to her. If you do not, how will you ever know whether your love is requited?"

Far from having forgotten the initial point of our discussion, she had now completely returned to it, and, if her grin was to be believed, she had been planning to do so all along.

"Neither Keith nor Mary are going to give up anytime soon, so why should you?" she went on, showing that she knew not only about my love, but also about that of her friends, who both happened to be in love with the same Katarina Claes. Her real calculating personality had shown through the facade of delusional ambition.

"But I am an adult now, and I shoulder the responsibility of succeeding my father as count," I said with a sigh. She already knew everything. There was no point in hiding the truth anymore.

"There are many adults who are not engaged, and I do not see why you should have to be forced to marry for the sake of your family's title," she responded dryly. This girl was not just a bit unique. She was *very* unique.

"I know that there are some who are still not engaged despite being of age, but marrying to preserve one's title is the norm for nobles."

"...Such an antiquated way of thinking."

As her words hit me once again, I realized that this girl showed absolutely no restraint in choosing them.

"And... a lot of people who are forced into finding a partner will ultimately be unhappy with their marriages," she continued.

"Forced into an unhappy marriage..."

Her grave expression reminded me of the incident that had taken place almost one year before, involving a friend of mine, who was a hard-working member of the student council.

The person at the center of it all was the wife of a marquess who had been cast away by her husband, and who lost her mind and eventually began meddling with Dark Magic. I did not personally know anyone in an unhappy marriage, but in our aristocratic society, where couples were routinely put together for strictly political reasons as had happened with the marquess, stories like that were common.

"And that is why I say that you should not marry against your will. Think also of the poor wife whose husband loves someone else."

This point of hers was the one that most resonated with me. I had only considered my feelings, not those of the girl who would become my wife. Of course I intended to love and respect her, but... would I really be able to do it? My lack of interest in them was apparent to the girls after we had met only one single time...

"...You are right. I have been only thinking of me and my feelings, completely ignoring the other party. I would not have realized it without your help. Thank you," I told her, bowing my head in gratitude.

"As long as you have realized it, there is no problem. And you did not only think about yourself. You also had your family in mind, after all," she said somewhat awkwardly.

My family? Of course... My parents brought me up with love and kindness, and I deeply respect them. If I wanted to marry and succeed Father as count as quickly as possible, it was also for their sake. But...

"That, too, is fundamentally for my own sake. It was *I* who wanted to make them feel happy and relieved," I said to the girl, who started giggling again.

"You really are as diligent as they say! But does your family really want you to meet lady after lady in a rush to marry?"

"...Well..." *I don't know.* When I first told Father about my intentions, he had indeed seemed vexed.

"Your priority should be confirming that with them, should it not?" she said with a smile, bringing an end to that discussion.

We then kept talking a while longer about the academy and other harmless topics before parting ways, because, as she said, "meetings too long or too short both cause their own problems." She was obviously much more used to matchmaking dates than I was.

I raised a hand to call on the servants, who were far away from us. But before they could reach us, she spoke again.

"You are keeping your love a secret from everyone, are you not? If you ever feel the need to talk about it, I will be most glad." Her smile had a hint of malice, like a child whose prank was successful.

"..."

I stumbled in finding a response, and, having put her mask of noble innocence back on, she said her farewells with the elegance of a proper lady.

Thus ended my meeting with this very unique girl.

My peculiar encounter with that girl had made me reflect on many things, so as soon as it was over, I spoke to my father.

"I'm sorry for doing this despite having asked for it in the first place, but I would like to take a break from the matchmaking meetings for a while."

He looked relieved, and said, "Of course! You're still young, and there's no rush. I'm sure that one day you'll meet the right person."

His reaction was so unlike him that I had to make sure.

"Will that really be alright? Shouldn't I look for a wife to succeed you as count as soon as possible?"

"Is that what worried you? There's no need to sacrifice yourself that much for something so petty in this day and age. If you don't care for the title, we can always adopt someone from our relatives to inherit it," he replied with a heartfelt laugh. Then he concluded, "Nicol, you really are every bit as diligent as your mother!"

After how much I had worried about having this conversation, the actual turn of events proved disappointingly anticlimactic. That girl was right. What my family really wanted was different than what I thought.

I really respected my father, an individual talented enough to be chosen as the king's counselor... but the laid-back view he shared with me today showed that he actually had a far laxer personality than I thought.

I had always wondered who Sophia had gotten her act-first-think-later mentality from, but perhaps I had finally found the culprit...

I was going to my room after having spoken with Father, but Sophia stood menacingly in the hallway, blocking my path.

"I heard that you were meeting potential fiancées! Why wouldn't you tell me?!" she said, visibly angered. She had heard about my matchmaking meetings from somewhere.

Was it the girl from today? But we only just parted ways. That would be surprising.

I asked her how she found out, and she told me that, worried about my recent unusual behavior, she had gone to Father for an explanation. Knowing how soft he was with her, the fact that he immediately told her the truth came as no surprise.

"Well...?" she said resolutely, as if threatening to block the hallway until I gave her all the details, which I promptly did.

I told her how I had felt the pressure of having to find a wife in order to succeed Father as count, especially because I had received several remarks about my lack of a fiancée since I had started working.

Sophia listened carefully until I was done talking, before commenting in the same way as Father had: "You really are diligent, huh!"

They resemble each other so much...

"Father told me the same thing. And also that I could just wait for the right person. You wouldn't expect a count to say something like that..." I said.

For some reason, my sister seemed surprised. "What? You expected Father, of all people, to tell you to marry for the family's sake?"

"What do you mean?"

"How could he say something like that, when he himself fell in love at first sight with an already engaged girl and then took her from her fiancé?"

This was the most surprising thing I had heard today, if not one of the most surprising things I had heard in my entire life. So much so that I couldn't utter a response.

"You... You didn't know?"

She had said it so innocently that I became dizzy from the shock.

"Wait, is that true? Did Father really take Mother from...?" Saying it myself made me feel even worse.

Father... taking her from her fiancé...

The two of them had always been so close with each other that I had been embarrassed to watch them as a child. But I would have never thought that their past could be made into one of Sophia's romance-triangle novels.

"Yes. Mother was engaged to another man, but Father fell in love with her and went to Grandfather to ask for her hand. Grandfather refused and told him, 'I'll let you marry my daughter the day that you become counselor to the king!' Of course he was only taunting him, but Father actually went and became counselor. So Grandfather admitted that he was worthy of Mother."

I did know that he rose through the ranks incredibly quickly, but I had never suspected that Father had become counselor so that he could marry Mother. Then again — *I'm feeling even dizzier* — of all possible reasons, actually... wait, more importantly...

"...Is that common knowledge? Why have I just heard this story for the first time?" I had spent eighteen years in this household and not once had I heard of my parents' romantic history.

"Naturally, Father took all the precautions he could so that the story wouldn't get out to the public. After all, stealing a girl from her fiancé is not something you want to advertise. But if you ask Mother, she'll be more than happy to bore you with the details... although I'm sure that she has removed anything even remotely negative about Father from her memory..."

If Father had taken precautions, that story would surely never be heard outside of this house. But what about Mother? My calm, reserved mother, passionately recounting her past with Father? I let out a long sigh.

Hearing for the first time the outlandish story of how my parents met each other had made my head hurt. Sophia, who had been furious moments ago, was now smiling at me.

"I thought that you knew everything, but I guess there are some things that even you don't know!" she said, obviously pleased about being able to patronize me for once. "If there's anything more you want to know, just ask me!" she added proudly, with an annoyingly satisfied expression.

I felt the respect I had always held for my father was in risk of waning ever so slightly.

After that, I stopped looking for a fiancée. And, for some reason, I felt that perhaps reading through one of those weird novels that Sophia always recommended to me, with words like "stolen love" in the title, wouldn't be so bad of an idea.

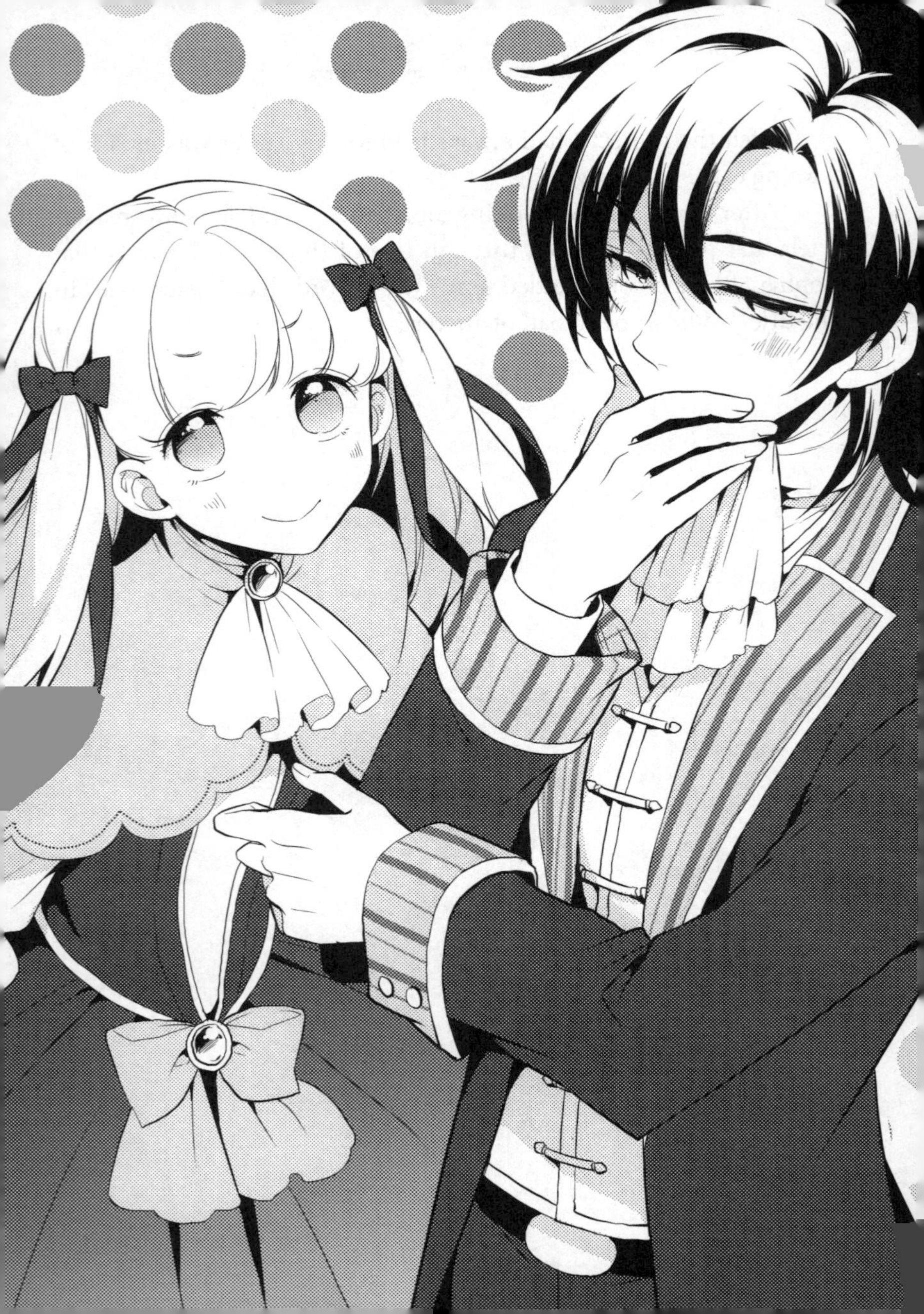

Almost a year had passed since I had started working at the Magical Ministry. It had been arranged for me to come here because of my involvement in some serious incidents, but, owing to the complicated nature of my past, everyone actively avoided me.

"Nobody wants him in their department? What a waste of a rare specimen! Well, then I'll gladly accept Raphael Wolt into mine!"

These were the words with which my superior, Larna Smith, accepted me into her department.

Larna, one of the leaders within the Ministry, was an all-around talented woman and an expert in disguise. Nobody knew what she actually looked like, or even where she had come from, making her stand out as an anomaly in a place where everyone was an anomaly to begin with.

However, she had many enemies due to her peculiar position, which meant that her department — which was my workplace as well — was often the subject of harassment. Talented as she was, she already had to take on a lot of work... and then some people would push even more onto us because they didn't like her.

"...Raphael, I'm spent... Mind if I sleep for a bit?"

"No! If you sleep now, you won't wake up for at least two days. Please... just a bit longer." I implored my overworked colleague to stay awake. The only answer he could muster was a sigh, and he looked as if he could fall asleep any second.

This won't do. I offered him a glass of cold water. "Here, drink this," I said, and he accepted it and started drinking in an attempt to stay awake.

As I continued working, the door opened and another overworked colleague, who had gone to wash his face to fight the drowsiness, came back in. He must have scrubbed really hard, as his face had turned red.

"So? Did you see Larna?" I asked him, to which he shook his head. Disappointed, I let out a sigh.

After the happy ending to the kidnapping of Keith Claes, a duke's adopted son, she came back to the office looking very pleased. But before long, she had gone off again to who-knows-where.

And what a time she had chosen to do so. Between the aftermath of the kidnapping and the work pushed onto us by the other departments, we were all exhausted and could think of only one thing: sleep. If she were here, she could make quick work of a good share of all this paperwork. We all wished that she would come back as soon as possible.

My boss was a truly talented individual... but she was also a very eccentric one. The second her interest was caught by something, she'd go off chasing it herself. That being said, she protected her subordinates, took responsibility for what she did, and was an all-around reliable and respected figure.

I should have made her stay here. But who'd have thought she'd disappear again so soon? I sounded my regret by means of yet another sigh. But there was no time for idle grief, so I made sure to keep working while I sighed.

My hands silently moved from one document to the next. It felt as if I was never going to finish. My vision and my thoughts both started to blur. I was getting close to my limit.

After three days of sleepless work, one of my colleagues — in a bout of something I can only describe as insanity — had concocted a dubious formula he called an "anti-sleepiness drink." If push came to shove, I'd have to consider drinking whatever that was.

As my blurred hands kept moving through the papers, my thoughts were interrupted by the sound of the opening door. The only member of the department outside the office, at that moment, was Larna.

Did she come back?! I thought to myself, elated, only to be disappointed to see Sora, the young man who had recently joined the Ministry. Larna had taken him under her wing, but before he could be taught the ins and outs of work in our department, she had brought him with her on a "research trip."

Normally we would have to teach him from scratch, but right now we could not spare the time to sleep, let alone teach anything to anyone. Therefore, we told him to go to the Ministry's library and study by himself, like one would do at school.

However, since he was involved in Keith's kidnapping, I had also asked him to write a simple report on that. That was likely the contents of the papers in his hands.

"Here is the report you asked me to write," he said, confirming my theory and handing me the papers.

"Well done, thank you."

He looked a bit distressed. "This is my first time writing an official document like this… I did get it checked, but…"

"Uh? Checked? By whom?"

All other members of his department were in this office, staring at their desks with bloodshot eyes. Did he ask someone from another department…?

"Oh, that would be Miss Smith."

"…Larna? Where is she?" I asked him as my heartbeat steadily got faster.

"I met her while coming here from the library," he answered, unaware of the trouble we were going through.

"So she was… here… Where exactly did you see her?"

"Hmm, it was right when I left the library, I think…"

The fastest runner in the department, upon hearing that answer, looked at me for an instant before standing up, and I returned his gaze with an imploring one. He nodded, left the room, and went after Larna.

If we managed to catch her, our work could potentially end so much faster. Maybe tonight we could even sleep! *In a bed!*

The small flame of hope warmed my heart. *Did my vision get a little less blurry?* Newly motivated, I looked over Sora's report, which the higher-ups had asked to be submitted as soon as possible.

If Larna checked it, it should be fine… is what I thought, until I actually read it.

"…Say, Sora, what did Larna tell you after checking it?"

"She laughed and then said something like, 'I like how *peculiar* it is'… Is there anything wrong?"

This poor, confused guy probably meant no harm… but this was no way to write a report.

"*…and then Katarina Claes was going crazy, like, 'This dog is so cute!' And she kept yapping like that…*"

This is how downtown delinquents talk! And why did Larna just laugh and let this slide?! I'm going to be the one who gets in trouble with the higher-ups! How can he be this bad at writing?!

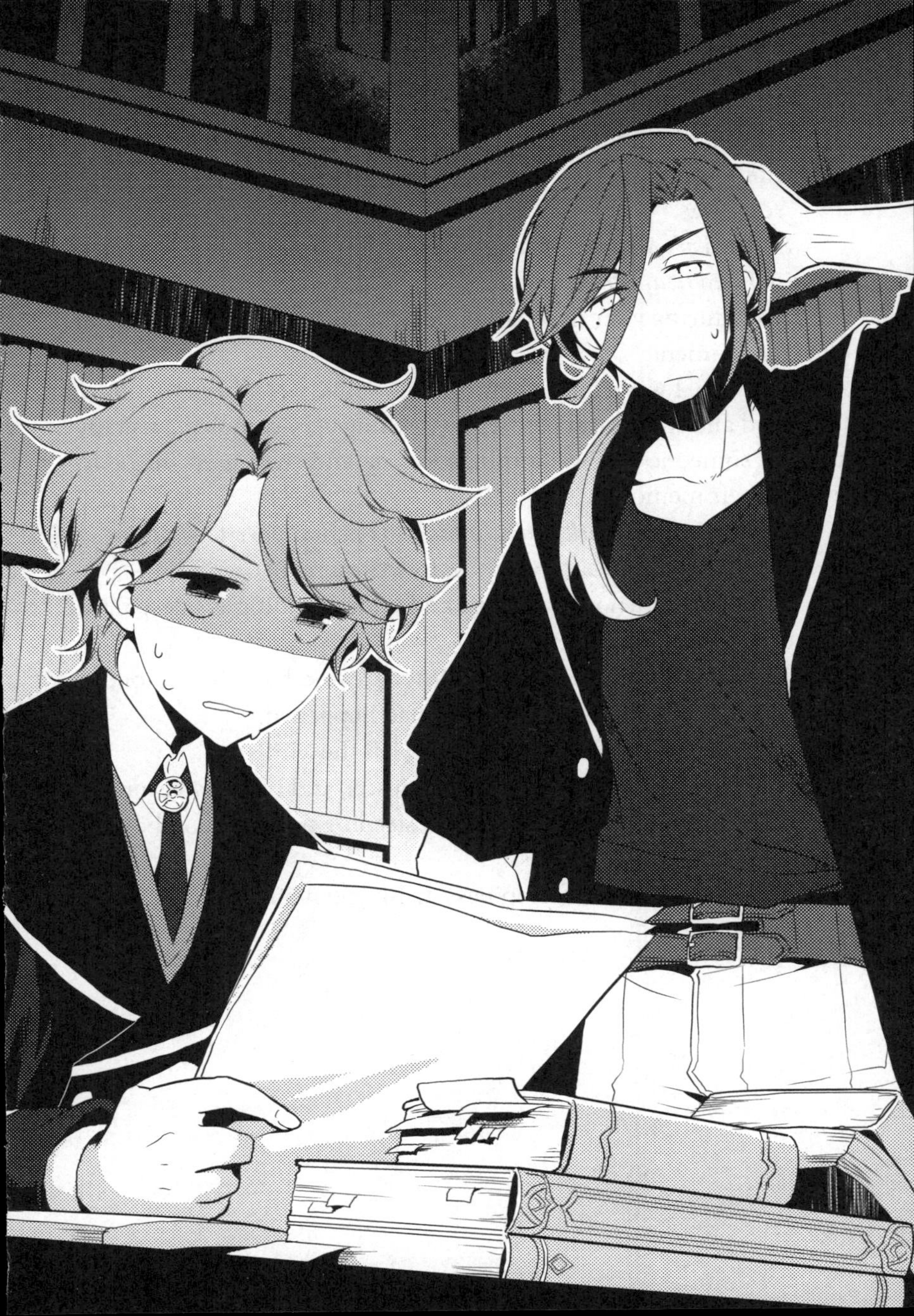

"…Sora, I heard that you used to be the butler for an important noble house, yes?"

"Yes, I was."

So I wasn't wrong. I felt safe letting him write this on his own because I had heard that, but…

"And, during your time as a butler, did you not write any kind of official document?"

"Oh, well, I was a butler but, you know, I've never been to school. I can read and write kind of fine, but nothing very complex. I usually just had someone else write things for me and then used magic to change their memories."

So he just used Dark Magic and didn't actually write anything…

"…I may have to teach you how to write a report…"

Sora gave me a nod of apology and understanding as I despaired at my work increasing even more.

The door opened and my colleague came back in… alone. I didn't even need him to explain what had happened.

"…I couldn't find her. She's already left the Ministry."

The whole department sighed in unison, and I felt my vision get even blurrier than before. My hopes of sleeping in a bed tonight were shattered.

"Hey, about that anti-sleepiness drink you made…"

The graduation ceremony that I'd been dreading so much came and went without incident, so by next spring, I would start my second year of studies. And with my worries gone, I was now free to enjoy myself.

The sun shone gently onto the garden, the birds sang happily, and more and more couples started walking around the academy together. It was as if the whole world had come together to celebrate Katarina Claes' success at avoiding all the Catastrophic Bad Ends.

I'm so happy... Uhm? Wait a second, why are there so many couples around?

"I heard that there always are more couples in spring," said my childhood friend Mary, answering that very question.

The other girls and I were spending the day in Mary's room, and the four of us were chatting together. Other than Mary and I, there was my other childhood friend Sophia and the *Fortune Lover* protagonist Maria, who had also become a good friend of mine.

During that pleasant all-girls tea party, I had voiced my confusion about what I had noticed lately. "Is it just me, or are there more couples than usual around the academy?" Which is the question that prompted Mary's answer.

"But why?" I pressed on. I was pretty sure they weren't actually celebrating my victory over the Catastrophic Bad Ends. Actually, ever since Jeord took me as his fiancée to avoid lady suitors, the only romance I'd experienced was in my books... *Are they doing this on purpose to taunt me?*

"It could just be the season. A lot of animals breed in spring. And also, most high-ranking nobles become engaged when they're still children, but the others start looking for fiancées after their debut in society, around the age that we are now. So these could be new couples, trying to get to know each other better."

So it's not about taunting me. That's good.

And, while I wasn't so sure what animals' breeding had to do with anything, the part about getting to know each other better seemed to make sense. A lot of them seemed to show that cute awkwardness typical of fresh couples.

"New engagements! New couples! Oh, it's so romantic!" said Sophia, who had also ignored the thing about animals.

"But I wonder... They're political engagements, aren't they? Is there really any romance in that?"

When Jeord proposed his engagement to me, my heart didn't race with love, but with fear over what I should do next. Sophia, romantic as usual, looked disappointed after hearing my unromantic view.

Mary noticed and tried to brighten the mood. "It seems that nowadays many young people are choosing their partners out of their own will, however."

"Really?" asked an excited Sophia.

"Yes. I've just heard of a lady who fell in love at first sight with a young man during her social debut ball. Struck by passion, she proposed to him."

"Love at first sight and a passionate proposal... It's so wonderful!" Sophia enthused.

"So even nobles marry out of love!" commented Maria in surprise.

Mary, well-informed on noble society as usual, explained that most marriages used to be political in the past, but that things were slowly changing now.

"Do you think the couples in the academy are of the love-marriage variety?" I asked her.

"Probably, yes," Mary replied after thinking for a moment. "They look pretty close."

If that were really the case, these would be the same type of lovers I used to frown upon with envy in my previous life. I had mixed feelings about seeing them enjoy their blooming youth like that. Before getting reincarnated here, I had only ever experienced love by proxy through my otaku media... Unfortunately, I died before I could ever go on a date with anyone.

And now in my second life, I was so busy dodging Catastrophic Bad Ends that, again, I had no time for romance. And the second that catastrophe was averted... couples everywhere. *Sigh.*

With four young girls getting together and chatting, you'd expect us to talk about love, but all we'd been talking about were topics like the vegetables in my field and the new dishes in the school dining hall. Why couldn't we talk about something more... *girly?*

The one romantic topic we did discuss was novels, but even then, Sophia had recently started liking ones geared towards more mature women, and you could hear her using words like "affair," "mistress," and other things you wouldn't expect a girl her age to say.

I finally realized that, just as in my previous life, I had been left behind in the race of love. But what about my friends? They were all incredibly beautiful, and with good personalities to boot. How could not a single one of them have romance in their lives? Or maybe they had partners, but hid them from me so that I wouldn't feel left out. The more I thought about that possibility, the more likely it seemed... and the sadder it made me feel.

"So… don't any of you have any romances going on?" I asked to fulfill my curiosity.

If they really were hiding their love stories out of consideration for me, I wanted them to stop. I just wanted to talk about romance like other girls my age.

It had taken some courage for me to ask about it so directly, but everyone just stared at me and tilted their heads, thinking in silence.

They really don't have any? Or are they keeping it from me?

"M-Mary, I mean, you're the focus of all the balls you go to… You must have a lot of boys approaching you!"

"…Approaching me?"

Katarina's stare had put me on the spot.

"But I am already engaged to Prince Alan…"

"Yes, but don't you ever get approached by a stunning boy at a ball?"

"…A stunning boy at a ball?"

Now that I thought of it, such a thing did occur quite often, despite the fact that I had a fiancé — Alan Stuart. It was only for show, but no one except me and the prince knew about this.

It was just last year that Alan, realizing his feelings for Katarina, suggested that we cancel our engagement. This did not surprise me, as I had always known that Alan was extremely candid for a noble. However, I refused and proposed that we stay formally engaged. Not because we had feelings for one another, but because it was just more convenient to do so.

Since he became my fiancé when we were eight years old, I had never disliked Alan; I was actually quite fond of his honest personality (which was a stark contrast with that of his cold, calculating twin).

But no one holds a place as large as Katarina in my heart. Had I not met her, I would have likely fallen in love with Alan — who was the closest person to me next to my family — and happily married him.

However, I had met someone unique and irreplaceable. A girl who changed me. A girl who saved me. I had never had feelings that strong for anyone before.

This was why I kept my engagement with Alan. The last thing I wanted was to marry someone and be forced to part with Katarina.

Despite this, for some reason, young men continued to approach me left and right. At first I was incensed, appalled that they would even come near a girl who was already engaged. But after attending many balls, I eventually realized that these people were not like the men in Sophia's novels, falling in love at first sight and passionately proposing, trying to take me away from Alan. They only sought the thrill of unfaithfulness.

In our noble society, that was far from the exception. Although this was slowly changing, the norm was for young men and women to be forced to marry for political reasons, often to someone that they had no regard for at all. They took this to mean that once they had fulfilled their duties by producing an heir, they could play around as much as they wanted. Nobles were much less loyal to their partners than commoners were.

As someone who was — to my displeasure — considered particularly attractive, I was the target of the advances of many such nobles.

Another reason for this could be the fact that I was not usually accompanied by Alan during the balls, even though he should have been my escort. (It was not that he would refuse if I asked him to, but attending solo was more convenient for snooping around…)

Usually, I would simply gracefully dodge the moves that any of those womanizers would try to put on me, but at the ball the other day I really risked getting into trouble…

The ball, a fairly large one, was close to its end.

"Come and keep me company! Just for a while!"

"Thank you, but I'm not interested."

This young man, reminiscent of a downtown thug, had been approaching me so insistently that both my voice and choice of words had become a bit rough from my annoyance. Failing to notice that, either because of innate stupidity or because of how much wine he had drunk, the boy continued to pester me with his breath reeking of alcohol. And, what's worse, he had somehow drawn me into a corner of the hall with no one around.

This isn't good… Maybe I should stomp on his foot with my heel and run…

"You've come this far… might as well play with me, no?" he said with a creepy smile as he pinned me against a wall. I could hardly move and was completely terrified.

"What d'you think you're doing to my fiancée?" said Alan, heroically coming to my rescue. He pulled my harasser away from me and stared at him menacingly. In response, he just stood there with his mouth open, trying to think of an appropriate excuse, before running away as fast as he could.

"Are you alright?" Alan asked me once I finally felt safe.

Taking a good look at him, I saw that he was out of breath. *He must have run here to save me as soon as he saw that I was in trouble,* I thought, and I couldn't help but smile.

"Thank you," I said, to which he blushed, turned away from me, and grunted a reply.

Perhaps he was childish, but I was glad to have him as my fiancé, even if it was just for show. And I wouldn't tell anyone that, on that day, I felt something for Alan that I had never felt before.

As for the harasser, I had him swiftly removed from noble society.

Even searching through my memories, I couldn't find any romantic stories like the ones that Katarina was looking for.

"…I do not believe I have had any episode of the sort…" I said, which made Katarina visibly disappointed.

Not without a hint of guilt, I passed the topic onto the friend sitting next to me. "Sophia, what about you?"

"Oh? …Me?"

"Yes, what about you, Sophia?" Katarina asked me with a sparkle in her eyes.

"…Well, I…" If Mary, a lady amongst ladies, didn't have a story that could satisfy Katarina… how could I?

To begin with, my situation was somewhat different from that of my friends. Because of my white hair and red eyes, I had always been seen as different, as an outcast. Before I knew it, I stopped leaving home for fear of the glances that people would throw my way.

It was only thanks to Katarina, who had praised my hair and eyes as beautiful, that I had started going out again. It was only then that I realized that not everyone looked at me with disgust.

That wasn't enough to completely undo my years of fear, of course, and I still attended parties and balls as little as I could. Unlike beautiful ladies such as Katarina or Mary, no handsome boy would ever approach me at a ball.

Just a few days ago, during the ball held by my relatives…

Attending a ball for the first time in so long, I was happy to be escorted by my beloved brother. Unfortunately, as he still wasn't engaged, he was one of the main targets for single ladies. He was snatched away by a group of avid girls as soon as he entered the hall, leaving me alone.

Katarina or Mary would normally be with me at balls, but in this small event hosted by an earl related to my family, I had no friends with me except for Nicol. The situation made me extremely anxious; I didn't like crowded places, I didn't like speaking with people I didn't know, and I didn't have the sociable personality to engage in conversation with just anybody.

I wanted to go home, but we had just arrived and I couldn't leave my brother alone. So I just found myself a wall to lean on and waited for him there, motionless, hoping that no one would see me.

I was enjoying the ball, in a sense. I looked at the other young men and women interacting and romancing each other… when I noticed something.

Someone was looking at me. It was a group of boys around my age sitting at a table far from where I stood. They were looking at me while talking to each other. Initially I thought that it was just my imagination, but our eyes met a few times, and I became sure that they were talking about me.

What are they saying? From this distance, it looks as if they're laughing. Are they laughing at how I look? I'm used to that sort of treatment; I have received it since I was little… The memories of my troubled childhood resurfaced, thoroughly killing any fun that I could have been having.

I should go home, I thought, when one of the boys from that table stood up and came walking towards me! Anticipating some insult along the lines of *"Someone like you doesn't belong at a ball,"* which I had heard time and again as a child, my whole body tensed up.

The boy reached me, and so that I could ignore whatever terrible thing he was going to say, I started thinking of the sweetest scene in my favorite romance novel. *So, the one where the prince falls in love with the lady at the ball and proposes to her on the spot. It went something like…*

"…Excuse me. S-Someone as beautiful as yourself does not have to stay alone by the wall. W-Would you not dance with me?"

I was able to imagine that scene so clearly that it felt as if the boy in front of me had actually said it. *My imagination really is incredible.*

But, as much as I would have liked to, I couldn't keep ignoring reality. After all, that boy was still standing in front of me… but what for? Had he insulted me already? I was so busy daydreaming that I hadn't even heard him.

His face was surprisingly red. *Is he ill?* "…Are you feeling al…" I tried to say, when my brother, who had finally freed himself from the swarm of fans, returned with a concerned expression.

"…Won't you reply to him?" he asked me.

"Reply? In response to what?" I replied. As the boy from before heard this, his face fell and he quickly retreated from the hall. "I wonder what was wrong with him…"

Nicol asked me to recount what had happened until now, and I explained that I had been pretending to be a piece of furniture when I was approached, and, fearing that I would be insulted, I began daydreaming (very vividly) to protect myself.

"I guess I must blame Katarina's influence for this," sighed my brother.

I had no idea what he was talking about, but I was happy that I had somehow been influenced by Katarina.

I tried searching my memories, including that ball, for any romantic story. But, unfortunately, I couldn't find anything.

"…I'm afraid I have nothing…" I said to a disappointed Katarina.

But if there was a girl who was sure to have some such story, it was the beautiful, popular, and talented Maria.

"Maria, what about you?"

"Oh? …Me?"

"Yes! A girl as pretty as you must get approached by boys all the time!" said Katarina, excited.

"…That's not really…" I mumbled, struggling to find an answer.

As a commoner, I was different from the nobles around me. I didn't attend balls like my friends did, so I didn't really have the opportunity for romantic encounters in the first place. A normal commoner would have such chances at school or work, but because of my magical powers, I always stood out… so much so that I had no friends, let alone love interests.

Now, chatting happily with my wonderful friends felt like so much of a miracle that I didn't really think of finding a boyfriend anymore. Of course, as the only commoner in the academy, the noble boys would never even take me into account.

It wasn't that I had no interest in love; I enjoyed reading the romantic stories in the novels that my friends recommended to me, and I thought that being part of one would be a wonderful thing. But I was so happy with my life that I hardly felt like asking for more.

Only a year ago, I'd had to withstand bullying and insults. But now that I had Katarina and the others to protect me, I had nothing to fear anymore. They were all high-ranking nobles, and they were all enthusiastically on my side, Katarina especially so. She was like a hero from a book, saving a tormented damsel… Where before there were bullies, now there were more and more kind people.

One day, I had stayed behind in the classroom after the lesson to ask a question regarding something that I had not understood. After that, the teacher asked me to help with bringing some heavy things to the dormitory. I agreed without thinking twice about it, but after a while I could feel my arms getting tired. I regretted accepting the task unconditionally… I should have told the teacher that I could only bring half of it at once.

"Hey, what are you doing with that?" asked someone from behind me.

I turned around to see a boy from my class. "I was asked to bring this to the dormitory…" I replied, and he silently took the weight off my hands and started walking towards the dorms. This all happened so fast that I was utterly confused, and I ran after him.

"E-Excuse me…"

"To the dormitory, right?"

"Yes… Thank you."

I had hardly ever spoken with him, and yet he was so kind to me. I thanked him with a smile and he bluntly muttered, "Sure."

We walked together for a while, and I offered to carry at least some of those heavy things myself, but he refused. Just as we came close to the dormitory, he suddenly asked me a question. "Say, Maria, are you… are you seeing anyone in the student council?"

"Seeing anyone? What do you mean?"

"Like, you know, d-dating anyone…" he explained, blushing.

"D-Dating?! N-No, I don't do anything like that…" I replied in flustered surprise.

"I see…" he murmured to himself, and then he went on, walking faster than before.

Actually, he had not been the first boy to be so kind to me as of late. Some would help me carry heavy things, just like he did, some would help me with my student council duties… They would all help me and then just disappear.

I came up with a theory as to why this was happening: Katarina and the others in the student council were very kind, and as they represented the whole academy, the other students were influenced by them.

Not only were my friends, who were now in their second year in the student council, wonderful people, but they even made those around them better…

I tried to search my memories for anything that could be interesting, but, unfortunately… "I don't think I have any stories like that. Sorry, Katarina," I apologized.

"There's no reason to apologize! It's not a problem at all!" she hurried to say.

After hearing the replies of Mary, Sophia, and Maria, I could only sigh.

I thought that they were just being considerate by keeping quiet about their romantic lives, but it turned out that they really were in the same boat as me… which still, somehow, made me glad that at least I wasn't alone. If these three beauties couldn't find any love, it just made sense that I, with this villainess face of mine, couldn't either.

And a damsel in distress being saved by a hero rushing in to save her, being proposed to by someone who fell in love at first sight with them at a ball, being loved by an army of boys, and then being treated nicely by everyone could make sense in a novel, but it was too unrealistic to happen outside of books. The best we could do here was get together and talk romance.

I was relieved to know that everyone around me was as unfortunate with love as I was. Tomorrow I'd be able to focus my energy on tending to my field, as usual, as the couples breezed by.

Satisfied, I ate another cookie.

Working as the Claes Family's Gardener

Many a winter had passed since I had started working as a gardener for Duke Claes. I was born in a poor village to the name of Tom Wisley, and for as long as I can remember, I was sent from one house to the next to work as a servant. What with my rugged face and my dislike of talking, I never made any friends and I always worked alone.

I was good with my hands and good around plants, so when I was still young, I started fixing gardens for nobles, merchants, and other rich people. After a while I turned into a fine gardener, but I still was bad at dealing with people. Some folks would trick me out of my pay, and sometimes even raise their hands against me.

And then, one day, I met that boy. He looked about the same age as me, but much more handsome.

"Are you the one tending to this garden?" he asked me all of a sudden, after I had just finished working on the plants around a noble's house.

I could tell from his clothes that he was of a higher class than me, so I started to pay all the normal homages…

"There is no need for that. So, this garden. Are you the one tending to it?"

I had done my best that day, as I always did, but now I was scared that there was something wrong with my work. "…Yes," I told him with a nod, and his eyes started sparkling.

"This house's garden has always been appallingly tasteless, but it is unrecognizable now! You really are gifted!"

"...Th-Thank you very much..." His stare was so intense that I didn't know what to do.

"Do you work exclusively for this house?"

"...No, they just hired me for a one-time job."

"So do you normally work for another family?"

"...None in particular."

I couldn't get people to like me enough that they'd take me in to work for them exclusively, so I hopped from one garden to the next.

Then the boy got all worked up and said, "Then come to my home! You shall be my gardener!" He brought me to Claes Manor, and years later, that very boy became the head of that manor.

He'd hired me kind of willy-nilly... but I really liked working here. The other servants were nice people, I had regular pay and vacations, and the duke was kind and forgiving. Everyone loved him! I was still bad with people, and I couldn't open myself up to the others working in the mansion... but the duke would come to me casually and ask me to go with him to hang around town in disguise.

We went to do it once, and he liked spending time with me so much that we did it again and again after that. Before I realized it, he'd started calling me "friend." Me! A lowly servant! At first I thought that it wouldn't be proper to do the same, but after a while I ended up calling him "friend" too.

I wasn't good with people, and I was bad at talking... So he was the first to call me that from the bottom of his heart. I wanted to always stay by his side, and I worked as hard as I could. Eventually, I was even appointed head gardener.

...And then, my friend became ill and died.

After that, my days felt empty. Nobody would come and praise my garden enthusiastically like he always had. I didn't go to town anymore… The downtown we used to go to together.

I want to go where you are… I want to see you again, my friend…

I even thought things like that, until she came.

"I want to build a field in this garden," she said, with her fierce blue eyes, looking just like him.

And that girl started coming to see me day after day.

"Mr. Tom! I'm here!"

She talked with me, kindly and casually, like my old friend did. I had avoided going to town because the memories of him were too much to bear… but she asked me to accompany her "to buy materials for my projectiles!" and I found myself enjoying going there once again.

After meeting that girl, I didn't feel the rush to follow my friend anymore.

"My dear friend, I have to ask you to wait for me a bit longer after all. But when I do come to see you, I'll have a lot of stories about your granddaughter to share."

Working as the Claes Family's Head Maid

I was born as the first daughter of a relatively well-off merchant family, and I started working as a maid for the Claes family when I was sixteen.

My sisters were both talented and charming, and received plenty of marriage proposals. As soon as they were old enough, they both married; the older one took her husband into our family and the younger went to her husband's family.

But I had none of the talent nor the social ability of my two sisters. My face made me look stern, and my voice made me sound angry — I had trouble finding friends, let alone lovers. Even after I finished my lonely years at school, I still didn't receive any marriage proposals like my sisters had.

I thought that I'd probably be alone all my life if I stayed home, and I'd just be a nuisance for my parents. I decided to go to work for the Claes family, which had always been close to mine.

It didn't take me long to realize that I wouldn't be able to enjoy a marriage and family like other girls, so I focused my energy on work. Unlike the others around me, my work was all I had. After about ten years, my work was rewarded when I was unexpectedly given the position of head maid when the previous one retired.

I was scared that people would treat me lightly because of my young age, so I put even more energy into my duties. With this face, this voice, and this relentless attitude, I had caused the maids and other servants to avoid me altogether. But I didn't stop giving my best, working to make the most out of my lonely life.

Despite my appearance, I liked frilly dresses, cute dolls, fairy tales with beautiful princesses, and adorable little sweets. People had laughed at me because of this ever since I was a child, and so I eventually started enjoying them only in secret.

My aura of austerity was so strong that my colleagues just assumed that I didn't like sweet things and wouldn't offer them to me. So when I had some free time, I would bake sweets myself, careful not to be seen, and eat them all alone…

A few years ago, before I was head maid, I had brought my secretly baked treats into the garden where I could sit and eat them by myself.

One of the other maids had recently married and left the mansion. While staring at the grass in front of me, I thought about how I was now just going to see one colleague after another leave me behind.

I'm not particularly talented nor likeable, so it's just obvious that I can't get married, but... Their happy smiles... I'm so envious of them... If only a fairy would come out of nowhere, turn me into a princess, and bring me before a handsome prince like in the fairy tales I read as a child...

I was busy daydreaming when I saw someone come out of the tall grass. It was not a fairy, but a little girl covered in leaves. This girl — a duke's daughter — stared at the sweets I was holding, silent except for the growling of her stomach.

"...Would you like some?" She was staring at me so hard that I couldn't help but offer her something.

"I can have some?! Really?!" she said, looking so excited that she could have been jumping up and down.

She ate some of my sweets, and despite the fact that they were the work of an amateur, she took a liking to them — so much so that she would seek me out sometimes to ask for them.

Unlike my colleagues, she never seemed scared or cold around me, and I, too, felt at ease around her.

Once she turned fifteen, she had to go to the Academy of Magic, and her personal maid, Anne, would follow her there.

I also wanted to go to the academy with her... but as head maid, I could not leave the mansion. This made me feel incredibly lonely.

A few days had passed since the young miss left the house.

"Excuse me," said a voice behind me as I sat in the garden, eating sweets by myself.

Nobody but Katarina usually came here, and she was at the academy right now... so who could it be? I turned around and saw one of the boys that had been working as gardener for the Claes family for the last few years.

He was tall for his age and had an earnest, loyal personality, making him popular amongst the maids. I'd often seen them chat him up, but I'd never talked with him myself.

"...Yes?" I asked, confused.

"Well... I... I really like sweets, and actually, I've eaten some of the ones you made. The young miss shared them with me. I really loved them, and... Could I maybe... have some?"

"...Oh, of course," I said to the blushing boy in front of me, also blushing myself.

I offered him a few of the confections, and he took them with the brightest of smiles.

Eventually, the dream of marrying and having my own family — the one that I'd given up on — came true. But that was a few years later.

The tales I had read as a child were true. That day, the girl who came out of the grass to meet me in the garden really was a fairy, using her magic to bring me happiness.

At the Ladies' Club

My name is Milidiana Claes. Last spring, my daughter Katarina — the main source of my headaches — left for the Academy of Magic.

127

My house regained its peace, and the wrinkles that had accumulated on my forehead over the past years slowly began to disappear. I did not receive any troubling communications from the academy, and therefore I believed that even a child as problematic as mine had managed to grow up now that she was attending school.

When she came back for summer vacation, she began tending to the fields and practicing throwing her strange toys, as usual. But as long as she behaved at the academy, I thought that I could forgive her abnormality at home.

But... I had been naive... Terribly so.

Today was the monthly tea party of the Noble Ladies' Club. This club was composed of several women from the highest ranks of nobility, some of whom were the mothers of boys and girls who were attending the academy and currently home for the summer. Considering this, it was only natural that our conversations that day would revolve around the school.

I listened to the stories that the ladies had heard from their children, while offering some of the stories that I had heard from mine. It was then that I heard about *that* rumor.

"I heard from my daughter that someone has made a field inside the academy's grounds!"

"A field? As would be in a farm?"

"Yes, indeed. And what's more, it would seem that it is a student who is responsible for this."

"Oh my!"

I tried to match the surprised expressions of the other ladies, carefully hiding the fear that had started creeping up inside of me.

"...But most of the students are from high-ranking families. It would be hard to believe that one of them would do something like that."

"Indeed! One of the children must have invented this rumor as a joke."

"That is most likely so."

"It still is a very ridiculous idea, is it not?"

The others were laughing, and I joined them. "Ridiculous indeed," I said with a smile. All the while, cold sweat was chilling my back...

Among that collection of noble children, who would ever think of playing farmer? The very thought was no doubt worthy of laughter. But my mind went to the field slowly taking over the Claes Manor garden... and to Katarina, happily tilling the soil...

I had believed that, at least at the academy, she was behaving properly. I had been wrong.

Just wait until I get home...

I clenched my fists below the table.

At the Academy of Magic

Wielders of magic from all over the country must enroll at the Academy of Magic once they turn fifteen. I was no exception — I was the daughter of a baron living far from the capital, and at the age of six, I used magic for the first time.

I entered the academy last spring. But as I came from a countryside family, I didn't feel at ease amongst the other, higher-ranking nobles. Had my magic been particularly powerful, my academic performance stellar, or my appearance beautiful — or, maybe, had I been a Light Magic user, like Maria Campbell — then I could have kept my head high from the start.

Alas, my magic was weak, and I lagged behind in my studies. I was sometimes told that I had a very friendly face, but I'd never been called beautiful. I felt out of place.

When they found out that their daughter could use magic — a first in the family — my parents were overcome with joy. But once in the academy, the others looked down upon me for coming from a relatively poor family from the countryside, and even bossed me around like a servant.

After a few months, I already wanted to go back home.

...But then, something happened.

I was discreetly reading a book in a corner of the classroom — one of the romance novels that aristocratic society scorned. But I had loved them since before moving to the capital, and I had secretly brought them with me from home.

"Is that... a romance novel?"

I looked up at the person who had asked me that question, and found that it was someone of such a high rank that it was surprising that they would bother talking with the daughter of a poor country baron.

Katarina Claes was a duke's daughter, and she was engaged to a prince. She stood near the top of the country's hierarchy, and therefore, even as her classmate, I could not simply talk to her like I would with another girl my age. In fact, I had never spoken with her even once.

Surprised by being spoken to, I froze on the spot, confused. But she smiled at me.

"I like romance novels too! Would you like to chat sometime?"

I accepted her invitation, and before I knew it, I was regularly meeting with her to have tea and talk about novels. And once I started spending time with her, the others at the academy stopped looking down on me and treating me like a servant.

Katarina was a wonderful, incredible person. She had the confident demeanor of a duchess, but she never put on airs like other high-ranking nobles, and never looked down upon anyone. She was even kind to me, the lowly daughter of a baron from the country.

I eventually realized that Katarina had stolen my heart. When I watched her playing with dogs in the thickets near the academy, or tending to the plants in the garden, I was reminded of the saintly girls of romance novels.

I was so focused on admiring her that I fell down and got dirt on my dress. Seeing this, Katarina offered me her handkerchief.

"It would get dirty," I said, trying to refuse.

But she smiled at me and said, "No problem! You can keep it!"

I held that handkerchief to my chest, swearing to treasure it forever.

I didn't want to go back home anymore… I wanted to stay here, near Katarina, for as long as I could.

★★★★★★★

"Big Sister, what happened to that thing you used to wear on your head?"

"Oh, the kerchief? I gave it to a classmate."

"What?! You didn't make that classmate wear it like you always do, did you?"

"No, she fell down and her dress had got dirty, so I gave it to her to clean herself up."

"I see… *Phew…* Wait, why didn't you just give her your *hand*kerchief?"

"I used it to clean my hands after working on the field, so it was all dirty."

"Oh, I see... Hm? Isn't the hem of your dress a little frayed?"

"Yep, the other day I was in the thicket and I met my worst enemy... a dog. It bit the hem of my dress, but it was only a puppy, so I managed to chase him off!"

"That's... That's wonderful... Anyway, I'm glad to see you so full of energy, but try to tone it down while you're at the academy. A few days ago you were picking fruit from the trees in the garden and eating it, weren't you? This isn't home, so you can't eat anything that you find lying down on the floor..."

"But it wasn't lying on the floor! I got it from a tree!"

"You're missing the point... Keeping Mother in the dark is starting to become difficult, so please, try to behave."

"...Okay," I said with a half-hearted nod, and my brother sighed.

At the Ladies' Club, Again

"Your daughter really is wonderful, Lady Claes. A lot of students worship her and say that she is like a saint."

I was at the monthly meeting of the Ladies' Club, talking with the mother of a child who, like Katarina, was currently attending the academy.

I thought I had misheard her, but when I asked her to repeat what she had just said, I realized that this was not the case...

This must be a misunderstanding... She must be mistaking my child for someone else's.

I only had one daughter, and a very problematic one at that. So problematic, in fact, that I often wondered where I went wrong in bringing her up.

Despite being from a noble family — a duke's family, no less — she climbed up trees in her dress, tilled the soil while wearing a kerchief over her head, and ate things that she found on the ground.

Had I heard of a problem student who was known for her monkey-esque behavior, then sure… that would be my daughter.

There was no way that Katarina was thought of as a saint. And yet…

"Are you quite sure that it is *my* daughter you are referring to?"

"Of course. I am talking about Katarina Claes."

"My own daughter is actually part of the Katarina Appreciation Society," another lady added.

"…A-Appreciation Society?"

"Yes. Of course it is not an official organization, but it has quite a few members."

I was so shocked that my mouth fell open and I almost froze that way.

This is impossible!

An appreciation society? For that devilish daughter of mine? Who could appreciate that monkey? Are they sure it is not Keith they are talking about?

I am very sorry for Katarina, but looking at them objectively, Keith is much more talented and admirable, despite not being biologically related to me.

Knowing this, I asked again and again… but there was no mistake. Katarina was the one with a fan club. And all the things I heard about her sounded like they were about someone else's daughter.

She loves plants? She only climbs trees and picks fruit to eat…

Animals love her? I have only seen dogs bark at her and chase her around…

I could hardly believe that this was the Katarina I knew. Perhaps the way I saw her behave at home was only a facade, and her real self was a saintly, admirable lady.

Coincidentally, she was now at home for the summer. I decided that, after the tea party, I would ask her directly.

"Heigh-ho! Heave-ho!"

As soon as I came back home, I found Katarina with a kerchief on her head, loudly bringing down the hoe to the field.

Seeing her like that... I was sure that the ladies at the club must have been mistaking her for someone else. Moments ago, I had thought that perhaps she really had a proper, lady-like side to her... But not anymore.

"Huff! Heave-ho! Heigh-ho!"

Her appalling exclamations echoed through the garden of the venerable Claes Manor. Hearing that was enough to make me feel tired, and I elected to retreat inside.

Katarina... I know you cannot become the wonderful lady the rumors say you are, but at least... try to become presentable... Alone in my room, I let out a deep sigh.

Once Katarina came back from the field, I told her to stop those weird sounds of hers... but the next day, once again, the garden of the venerable Claes Manor echoed with the sound of "Heigh-ho!"

"Your daughter, today..." I was complaining about Katarina to my husband in our bedroom, as I often did.

"She's always full of energy, isn't she?" replied Luigi Claes with a smile.

He was handsome, kind, and talented; a truly wonderful husband. But he had one fault: When it came to Katarina, he was extremely soft. He loved her so much that no matter what incident she got herself into, he would laugh and forgive her.

He had better realize what kind of girl his daughter has turned into...

"It is nothing so endearing as her simply having too much energy... She is always so rushed, never stopping to think before she acts. Once she has her mind set on something, she never listens to those around her. Who did she get that personality from?" I said with a sigh, and Luigi looked at me as if wanting to say something.

"What is it?"

"...No, it's nothing," he said, so I continued to complain about Katarina for a while.

I still cannot fathom how she could grow up with a personality like that. That is what I thought as I fell asleep, and luckily, the words that my husband muttered by my side never reached my ears.

"Katarina didn't only get her face from you..."

Having Met You
～Keith Claes～

"I wish you were never born!"

"Why must that brat stay in my house?"

"Go away, you monster!"

Why? Why does everyone hate me?

Why doesn't anyone stay by my side?

I don't want to be alone.

I'm so lonely.

Please... Someone... Anyone. Stay with me.

135

I woke up and looked at the ceiling that, over the past months, I had become used to seeing. *That's right*, I thought, *this is Claes Manor. This is my family now.* I sighed in relief.

Ever since I was born, I had always been hated and treated like a nuisance. However, this was not the case anymore since I had come to Claes Manor. My kind family was happy to share their meals with me, and cared about me and my health. I had all that I had ever wished for.

And yet, I still sometimes had those dreams from the past. Dreams of being insulted and rejected. It should have all been behind me, but… it still made my chest hurt.

Today, I was supposed to attend a tea party along with my sister. With my chest still hurting, I started to prepare.

"Thank you for coming with me, Keith," said Katarina, smiling at me on the carriage that was to take us to the tea party. Her smile made me feel better.

"I'm bad at remembering faces, so going alone is a bit scary. I'm so happy you're here with me!" Her blue eyes were looking straight into mine. "Thank you for coming to our family, Keith. I'm so glad that I could become your sister."

Hearing these words almost made me cry. Happiness warmed my chest, that had been filled with pain from my dream, from the inside.

Katarina Claes is such a mysterious girl. She always says just the right thing at the right time.

"…I'm just as glad to be part of the Claes family and to have you as a sister," I told her, and she gave me yet another one of those kind smiles of hers.

I'm so grateful to have met Katarina, I thought from the bottom of my heart.

～Mary Hunt～

After first meeting Katarina, I spent the next few months trying to become a lady respectable enough to be worthy of her company.

I had to train in a wide variety of fields: academics, dance, etiquette, and more. With no particular talent, I was actually a slower learner than those around me, which is why none of this training went smoothly. I had to put in more effort than anyone else.

I studied all night, asking question upon question of my instructor whenever he was there. I practiced etiquette day after day until I finally managed to behave correctly in any situation. I worked on dancing for so long that I wore out my shoes and my feet began to bleed.

My half-sisters from another mother laughed at my efforts.

"Look at this talentless fool trying so hard!"

"A noble lady training so obsessively is nothing short of embarrassing."

"She is just as bad as expected of someone born from a low-ranking mother!"

These words felt like arrows piercing into my chest, poisoning it with pain.

But whenever I was with Katarina, the pain became lighter. And then, one day...

"Ouch..."

"Mary? What's wrong? Are you okay?"

As soon as I stopped walking and crouched down, Katarina worriedly called out to me. I had come to her house for a visit, and we were now going through the garden and to her field. My foot had suddenly started aching, and, taking a good look at it, I saw that it was bleeding slightly.

"Mary! You're hurt! Did you hit your foot somewhere?!" Katarina asked.

Influenced by her panic, I replied with a hint of panic as well. "…It's fine. Yesterday I practiced dancing for too long, and my feet are a bit worn out… that is all."

"Dancing?"

"Yes. I'm a bad dancer, so I have to practice harder than most people…"

I immediately regretted saying this. *Will she think that I can't even dance without practicing until my feet bleed? Will she laugh at me?*

Worried, I looked at Katarina. But her eyes held none of the contempt that my sisters' did. She was looking at me in awe.

"Working so hard to improve at something you're bad at… Mary, you're incredible. I should really learn from you!"

I gave my best day after day, only to be made a fool of. *"Why are you trying so hard?"* they asked, laughing at me.

But I didn't care anymore… because she was here. And she told me I was incredible for working so hard.

"Let's go back to the manor and tend to your wounds," said Katarina, dragging me by the hand. But I could only think of one thing:

I'm so grateful to have met Katarina Claes.

About Our Engagement

I called for my fiancée, Mary Hunt, telling her that we had to talk. We planned to meet in a private room in the dorm so that nobody would be around to overhear us.

I wanted to finally talk to her about something that I'd been thinking about for a long time. It'd been almost a month since Katarina was attacked with Dark Magic. We'd all been scared out of our minds, but in the end, she had been fine.

The guy who was behind it all, Sirius — or Raphael, I guess — left the academy, and work at the student council had been hectic for a while. But now things had gone back to normal.

And there was something that I absolutely had to do.

I, Alan Stuart, was eight years old when I got engaged to Mary, the fourth-born daughter of Marquess Hunt. She was cute and she worked really hard, and I liked her, but I started to realize that my feelings for her weren't romantic.

This happened because of the incident that had almost killed Katarina. When I thought of losing her, it made me realize that I was in love with her. And once those feelings started pouring out of my heart, I couldn't stop them anymore. All I wanted was to be by her side, and to see her smile.

Of course, I knew that she was already engaged to my brother. So my wish would never come true. But I still wanted to stay with her for as long as I could.

And then, while thinking about my feelings, I thought of Mary. I liked her, yeah, but it was more like brotherly love than anything romantic. Sure, that still *is* love, but… how would she take it? Would she be happy, married to a man who loves someone else?

After mulling over the problem, I decided to tell Mary the truth: that I loved someone else, someone who I wasn't allowed to love. I wanted her to decide what to do about our engagement. Whether to keep it or cancel it…

Finally, Mary came.

My lovely fiancée looked curiously at my grim expression. I didn't mention Katarina's name, but apart from that, I told her everything.

"Mary, I'm really sorry. If you want, I'll have the engagement canceled immediately, so that it won't bother you anymore."

At first she had been surprised, but then her expression looked irritated.

"...He is more earnest than I predicted. This is going to be such a pain..."

"What?"

Mary said something, but her voice was so low that I couldn't make out her words.

"Oh, it's nothing," she said with a smile. "I understand how you feel... but if we cancel the engagement, my family will surely pester me to enter a new one as soon as possible. And I would not want that."

"Why not? You're so popular that you'd have no problem finding a great husband that loves you."

There were actually a lot of men who'd jump at the opportunity if Mary canceled her engagement. But she shook her head with a grim look.

"No, that is out of the question... I have kept it a secret until now, but... My feelings, too, are for someone else."

"What?!" My jaw dropped in surprise.

"I'm sorry to have hidden this from you for so long... But my love is also a forbidden one."

"I see... We've been in the same boat all along..."

Who would have guessed that she loved someone else that she wasn't allowed to also? And how could I fail to notice that? *I'm so dense.*

"But I don't want to give up… The odds are against me, but I will give my best. Rather than having to deal with a new fiancé, it would be much more convenient for me to keep things as they are. Please, don't cancel our engagement," she said, on the verge of tears.

How could I tell her no, when she looked at me like that?

"Okay. Let's stay engaged until your love is fulfilled," I said, and her face lit up into a happy smile.

It was much later that I found out that this girl, with her lovely smile, was another rival… and a formidable one at that.

He Found Out About the Thing

"Say, Katarina. Why is your pocket always bulging? It has been bothering me for a while."

After having overcome the Catastrophic Bad Ends, I was leisurely drinking tea with Jeord, who asked me that question.

Uh? Do I have something in my pocket? I thought, sticking my hand inside it and taking out the contents.

It was a toy snake, the best one I'd built in the past eight years. I had put it in my pocket the other night to save myself from catastrophe, and I'd forgotten that it was there.

And I took it out in front of Jeord, of all people…

I threw one at him once eight years ago, and his retribution was so harsh that, ever since, I'd always made sure he wouldn't see me building them or practicing throwing them.

Why did I forget about it at a time like this?! I avoided a bad end, but it feels like I'm heading for another…

I clenched my fist around the snake, avoiding looking at Jeord's face. But without even looking, I could feel the tension building.

Oh no… I have to come up with something…

"Ah, wow! What is this, I wonder? Who would ever put something like this inside my pocket?"

Let's go with the old "someone put it in my pocket and I didn't notice" trick.

My delivery was so-so, but the idea, if I may say so myself, was brilliant. I would just pretend that this toy snake wasn't mine, and that someone had put it there as part of some kind of conspiracy.

"When did this get in here?" I said, continuing my spiel.

"What? Someone put it in there, and you didn't notice?!" asked Jeord, confused. His expression was as tense as his voice.

Yes! I fooled him! Not bad, Katarina, not bad. You could become an actress one day! Now confident in my acting skills, I pressed even further.

"Yes… Who could have done it?" I said with a distressed expression, feeling like a movie star.

"Who indeed, who could do something like this?" said Jeord, who I had tricked one hundred percent.

Phew. Crisis averted, I thought. But…

"…Is that what you really expected me to say?"

"What?!"

I looked at Jeord, whose voice had suddenly changed, and his face had the same evil smile of eight years ago when I had thrown the snake at him.

…Why? Hadn't I fooled him? I stared at him, confused, and he went on talking.

"How could you possibly not notice if someone put something in your pocket? And why would anyone do that in the first place?"

"…That's… true…"

Now that I heard him say that, I realized that my idea wasn't so brilliant after all. *Jeord really is a genius...*

"You are about the only one who could ever be fooled by a lie as silly as that!"

"..."

"And I had kept quiet about it until now, but I knew that you were making those *things* and practicing throwing them!"

"Wha?!" I'd done everything I could so that he wouldn't notice... but it was all in vain!

"So, would you care to explain why you were doing those things?" he said with the most charming of smiles.

"Well... that's..." I froze. I couldn't tell him *"To throw them at you when push comes to shove."*

"Well, I do have a general idea... What should I do now? Should I tell your mother about this?"

"No, please, anything but that..." I started panicking as Jeord's smile grew even more evil. *If Mother found out, I'd never hear the end of it...*

"I see... I will not do it, then... But you must do something for me in return."

"Of course! I'll do anything! Thank you!"

I survived! Whatever he asked of me, it could never be as bad as the scolding that Mother would give me.

Jeord brought his handsome face closer to me. "Tonight, by yourself, come to my room. And make sure that no one sees you."

"Hm? Why?"

I was expecting him to ask me to do his homework, or go buy his lunch, or something... Why did I have to go there without being noticed? Did he have some secret to share?

143

"You will find out why once you come. You said you would do anything, did you not?"

"Y-Yes…"

It really did sound like he wanted to share a secret with me. *I'll be happy to listen to him and help him out.*

"I am looking forward to seeing you tonight," he whispered into my ear with a questionable smile, and I felt a chill run down my spine. *I wonder why that is. Weird.*

While I was wondering about that chill, I felt someone dragging me to the side. I was surprised to see Keith there.

"Jeord… you are getting uncomfortably close to her."

"She is my fiancée; it is only normal that I would get close to her. You, on the other hand, should refrain from touching her so carelessly. Are you not a bit too old to be so attached to your sister?"

Jeord had replied to Keith's rough remark with a smile, but the next reply didn't come from Keith, but from someone else.

"Katarina is not yours yet, Prince Jeord… You still are not married," said Sophia, who had appeared out of nowhere with an angry look on her face.

"Indeed. You are simply engaged, and that may change at any moment!"

"What do you mean by that, Lady Mary?"

"I meant what I just said, Prince Jeord," said a smiling Mary to a smiling Jeord.

They all look so cheerful, smiling at each other… but for some reason, I felt like there was some tension in the air.

All the members of the student council had somehow come together around me, and they all looked mad. And I could still feel that tension in the air. *I thought I'd overcome the Bad Ends…*

"Katarina, are you done talking with Prince Jeord?" asked Mary menacingly.

"Uh? Oh, yes," I said, and she forcefully grabbed my hand.

"Let's go drink some tea somewhere else, then."

"Uh… sure."

I then had tea while chatting with Mary, Sophia, and Maria, and that weird chill in my back finally calmed down.

I wonder what that was… Did I catch a cold?

I didn't manage to get to Jeord's room that night, as Keith and the others found me out. They scolded me, and told me never to do something like that again.

They had a point… A lady shouldn't go to a man's room alone at night. *Next time I'll tell Jeord that I'll listen to whatever is troubling him during the day. But still, what is this weird tension between all of my friends? The Catastrophic Bad Ends were supposed to be a thing of the past…*

What Happened to the Thing

One day, when I was in town with my son, we passed in front of a store that was owned by an acquaintance who mainly traded in wooden containers and boxes.

"Oh! Dad, look at that! Wow! Can I have it?" said my son, pulling me inside by my hand.

The store was renowned for its product assortment and quality, and even served some noble families… Did it really sell anything that could catch an eight-year-old's eye?

Curious, I looked at what my son was pointing to, and saw… a snake.

At first I was startled to see it sitting there on the table, but when I took a better look, I realized that it was just a toy.

"Wow! Wow!" my son kept yelling, completely charmed by the thing.

That toy was really well made — anyone would have been fooled by it. We both peered at it, with my son crouching to bring his head level to the table and me standing behind him.

"Welcome," the shop owner greeted us.

"Hello," I replied, then asked about the snake that my son was so enamored with.

"I was visiting a noble family to sell them some goods and found it lying on a shelf. I praised its craftsmanship and one of the servants just gave it to me, saying that they have so many lying around that they don't know what to do with them," he explained.

"A noble family?"

Did some rich aristocrat carve this during a bout of bored lunacy? It looked too well made for that explanation.

"Dad! Can I have it? I can, can't I?" asked my son, his eyes twinkling at the lifelike toy snake.

After asking for the shop owner's permission, I picked it up. It was much lighter than I had expected, and for some reason, it was very comfortable to hold. It was almost as if it had been built to fit in one's hand.

After thinking for a while, I said, "Say, could I have this?"

"Sure. I got it for free to begin with," he replied instantly.

"By the way, where did you get it?" I inquired further.

"Duke Claes' mansion. Despite their rank, they're a really nice family, and all the servants are so friendly."

"I see… Duke Claes… And the servant that gave this to you said that they have a lot of these lying around, right?"

"That's right, but… why? Do you want more of them?" said the shop owner in surprise as I grinned.

"Exactly. Can't you see my son's face? Kids love a toy that looks just like a real animal. And it's light and easy to hold. They would make a killing if I started selling them!"

"Would they? Well, I guess if the town's top merchant says so, it must be true."

Indeed, I had quite the influence amongst merchants in the town, and — not to brag — I was also the one with the largest profits. Almost all of the new products that I started selling were hits. And my instinct told me that this toy snake would be, too.

"There's no time to lose! I have to go to Claes Manor!"

I left the shop, with the snake I had gotten for free in one hand and my son's hand in the other.

The more I looked at that toy, the more I realized how well it was built. The person who carved it obviously wanted to make it look as much as possible like a real snake.

But if they didn't want to sell them and just left them collecting dust… then why did they even build them?

"…ATCHOO!"

I suddenly felt an itch in my nose and let out a loud sneeze, and Keith, who was next to me, gave me a bothered look.

"Big Sister, that sneeze wasn't very ladylike…"

"What am I supposed to do? A sneeze is a sneeze," I said, sniffing.

Keith looked even more bothered than before and sighed, picking up the fruit of Grandpa Tom's and my labor from the shelf. "And by the way, Big Sister… what's with all these snakes? I'm seeing them all over the house lately. Why don't you throw them out already?"

"What?! Throw them out?! Grandpa Tom and I put our heart and souls into making them! I could never do that!"

"At least don't leave them around like this… Guests are weirded out by them."

"Well, I've made so many of them, but now I don't need them anymore… I just wanted to use them somehow!"

I thought that putting them away where no one could see them would be a waste, and so I placed them in the open, but… unfortunately, people didn't seem to like them.

At first I was praised for how well they were made, but now it was all "Get rid of them" and "They're a nuisance"… What a bummer.

Keith looked at my disappointed face, perplexed, and asked, "Why have you been building these in the first place?"

"…Well, that's…" I could never tell him that I was planning to throw them at Jeord, so I remained silent, prompting another sigh from my brother.

"Whatever the case, you should get rid of them. If Mother comes back home and finds toy snakes all over the place, you'll be in for one stern talking-to."

He was right… Mother had been out on vacation with Father for a few days, and she wouldn't be happy to find my masterpieces decorating the house. On top of that, I ended up breaking one of her favorite vases while I was laying the snakes around, so I couldn't just leave things as they were. I knew that, but…

"Aww… But throwing them out after all the months and years I've spent making them would be such a waste… I'd like to at least give them to someone…"

My poor toy snakes, stuffed away where nobody can look at them? That's too sad!

"…Yes, if there were anyone who would accept them," said Keith, giving me a blank stare.

At that time, I still didn't know that the same toy snakes that everyone in the house treated as a nuisance would become a hit in town.

The Start of Father and Mother's Romance

"Now that their third daughter has married into a good household, Duke Adeth must be elated."

"Indeed… However, not only has the second daughter yet to marry, but she is not even engaged yet."

"Is she not? Do you mean that her younger sister married before her?"

"Precisely. Rumor has it that the second daughter is not as sociable as her siblings, and has a rather stern face that drives suitors away."

"But she is not so young anymore… At this rate, she may become too old for marriage before she finds a fiancé."

"That is true, and it is the very reason why Duke Adeth is searching far and wide for someone to marry his daughter."

"To think that a duke's daughter would have trouble finding a man! Poor Duke Adeth, he must be so embarrassed."

"I am sure he is!"

The two ladies' tone had more than a hint of mockery to it. I left the room, taking care not to be noticed by them.

I am Milidiana Adeth, Duke Adeth's second daughter. Today was the day of the party celebrating my younger sister's marriage.

Among the many words of congratulations, one could hear remarks like the ones the two ladies had just made, making the party a very uncomfortable place for me to be.

I was much more shy than my siblings, and my face looked, as people remarked behind my back, as if I were always scoffing at everyone. For these reasons, I still was not engaged, let alone married.

My father, as duke, insisted that I marry someone worthy of my rank. But all the candidates he found for me routinely fell for my sisters, who were much more talented and sociable than me.

Despite all this, my family, far from treating me as a bother, was very kind to me. My mother and siblings would always stand up against anyone who insulted me, and my father was still looking for someone who would marry me. But being treated so kindly made me feel even worse about myself.

If only I had the kind smile of my sisters, I thought in disappointment as I found myself grimacing at today's party. Just being there filled me with sorrow. Had the one being celebrated not been my beloved sister, who would always side with me, I would have already said that I did not feel well and left.

I sighed and moved towards a corner of the room, planning to hide until the party was over, but the hall was suddenly filled with excited voices. I looked at where the excitement was coming from and saw a man, who had likely just arrived — late.

The voices belonged to the ladies swarming around him. Curious, I walked closer to discover the reason for so much fuss.

He was incredibly, stunningly handsome. His shiny golden hair and blue eyes made him look like a prince from a fairy tale. I reacted to seeing him in much the same way as the other ladies: by blushing and staring.

"He is so handsome!"

"Who is he?"

"You do not know him? He is Luigi Claes, from the duke's family!"

"He is *that* Luigi?"

I overheard the man's identity... Luigi Claes, heir to Duke Claes. Even someone as unsociable as me, who seldom attended balls and had few friends, knew of his name. He was beautiful, charming, smart, and talented... and, as if that was not enough, he was destined to become duke. No other man was as sought-after as him in aristocratic society.

A single glance was enough for me to fall for him, but now that I knew who he was, I could never approach him. My rank may have been high enough, but someone as beautiful as him seemed to come from another world than I, a girl whose unapproachable personality had kept me unmarried.

I managed to tear my eyes away from him and tried to move back to the corner I had come from.

"Milidiana!" called out a voice from behind me.

It was my father, wearing a wide smile on his face. And beside him was... Luigi Claes?!

I was paralyzed with surprise, but Father gestured for me to come to them. To be honest, I did not want to go so near the center of the hall, nor near someone who gathered as much attention as Luigi... However, I could not pretend that I had not noticed my father, so I begrudgingly obliged.

"Luigi, this is Milidiana, my second daughter."

"I am Milidiana Adeth. It is a pleasure to meet you," I said, in the most ladylike fashion I could manage.

"I am Luigi Claes. The pleasure is mine. Your father has always been very kind to me," he replied with a smile so charming that it made all the ladies around us sigh. Of course, after sighing, they shot me their coldest stares...

He was even more handsome up close... As his blue eyes looked into mine, I felt my face becoming hot.

And the scariest thing was that he was so attractive that when he told me, "You are truly beautiful, Lady Milidiana," I felt like passing out despite knowing that it could be nothing but empty flattery.

For reasons I did not understand, Luigi ended up spending the rest of the party with me. My father had probably asked him to do so — it would not be good for the host's daughter to be alone against a wall the whole time — and he had complied, repaying whatever favors he had received previously.

At first, I felt uncomfortable being stared at with hate by the ladies who wanted to enjoy Luigi's company, but then I realized that I would never have another opportunity like this and forgot about them.

Once this party is over, he will probably never even look at me again... I might as well enjoy my time with this fairytale prince while it lasts.

And enjoy it I did, as happy as I had ever been.

"Milidiana, I had a lot of fun with you today. Let's see each other again," he told me with a smile when we parted.

Enchanted, I replied, "Of course."

But I knew that we would not meet again.

...Or so I thought.

"Wh-What did you just say, Father?" I asked in a daze.

"As I said, your engagement has been decided, Milidiana. It was Luigi Claes who asked for your hand. Quite the wonderful news, don't you think?"

"Luigi... Claes..."

I listened to my father, but what he was saying was so difficult to believe that I could not process it. Luigi? Asking for my hand? Why would someone as popular as him do such a thing?

As I was still too shocked to comprehend the situation, time passed and the preparations went so far that the date of the wedding had already been decided.

I was madly in love with Luigi, but I did not know why he would ever stay by my side and give me the kind words that he did... until the other ladies from high society told me.

"Luigi has been treated very well by the Adeth family, so he took the leftover daughter to repay the favor."

"He has such a strong sense of duty, he must have felt obligated to help them!"

"It is so sad that such a wonderful man would have to marry such an undesirable girl."

Their words cleared up all of my questions. *Luigi married me to repay my father's favors...* After all, the first time we met, he did say, "Your father has always been very kind to me."

That's why he married me... out of obligation...

But, even after knowing the truth, my feelings for him would not disappear... Still torn between happiness and sadness, I became Milidiana Claes.

Luigi was always very kind to me, but, maybe because he had only taken me as his wife out of duty, I could feel some distance between us.

I love him… but he does not love me back. The more he was kind to me, the more I fell in love with him… and the more painful it became. Even after our daughter was born, things did not change.

However… when our daughter was eight years old, we adopted a child to be our son. Then, after a series of incidents, I finally realized that we had been misunderstanding each other all along.

He had not married me out of obligation, but had loved me from the start. The pain I had felt in my chest for all these years disappeared at once. We were finally able to feel like a married couple for the first time.

At last, I was happy from the bottom of my heart.

"Heigh-ho!"

We now loved each other more than ever, and our days together were as sweet as those of two newlyweds.

"Heave-ho!"

Our adopted son was also smart and talented, adding to my happiness.

"Heigh-ho!"

…What's this sound?

I was drinking my afternoon tea, savoring the moment as I remembered the past… but these weird sounds coming from the garden were ruining the atmosphere.

There was only one person who would yell like that in this respectable, venerable family. I put my tea back onto the table and made for the door leading to the garden. Once there, I found that the noise had come from the person that I had expected, who was tilling the soil in the getup that I had also expected.

Because of *that person*, the beautiful Claes garden was slowly turning into a field.

"Heigh-ho! Heave-ho!"

I approached *that person*, who was so concentrated on working the hoe that she did not even notice me.

"*Katarina!*"

The only daughter of Duke Claes.
Has angled features that make Katarina herself feel that she looks like a villainess. Has been fighting valiantly to avoid Catastrophic Bad Ends after regaining memories of her past life and realizing that she has been reincarnated as the antagonist of an otome game.

Katarina Claes

Likes	✦ Delicious food, romance novels
Dislikes	✦ Anything involving academics
Element	✦ Earth
Special Skills	✦ Agriculture, tree climbing, Dirt Bump
Personality	✦ Honest, simple, dense

Q

Is there anything you would like your lover or marriage partner to do for you?

Being held like a princess like in those romance novels, having them whisper sweet nothings into my ears in a place with a beautiful night view... or so I thought. Lately, though, I've discovered that hearing sweet nothings in my ear is way too intense! This is a lesson I've learned the hard way.

Power Gauge

Wisdom

Stamina

Power

To some people

Magic

Charisma

Third crown prince of the kingdom, and Katarina's fiancé. Although he looks like a typical fairy-tale prince, he secretly has a sadistic and scheming nature. He spent most of his days in boredom until he met Katarina. Ever since then, his love for her has grown year by year.

Likes	◆ Interesting things
Dislikes	◆ Slim and long animals
Element	◆ Fire
Special Skills	◆ A genius – he can do anything.
Personality	◆ Secretly a sadist

Q

Is there anything you would like your lover or marriage partner to do for you?

For her to ask me to spoil her.
Perhaps for her to smile by my side, that would be quite pleasant as well. At the very least, that is what I would say on the surface... but there are many other things. However, this is not quite the place for it. We could discuss it after a change of scenery, if you would like?
Ah, that is not necessary, you say? Most regrettable.

Jeord Stuart

Power Gauge

Wisdom

Stamina

Charisma

Magic

Power

Character Profiles

Jeord's twin brother and the fourth crown prince.
Handsome but wild and untamed, Alan is a prince who is
rough around the edges. Very good with instruments
and said to be a musical genius.
Although he originally had a complex towards Jeord,
he eventually conquered it thanks to Katarina.

Likes	◆ Instruments, musical performances
Dislikes	◆ The dark political undercurrents of noble society
Element	◆ Water
Special Skills	◆ Ability to play any instrument
Personality	◆ Boorish, somewhat dense

Q

Is there anything you would like your lover
or marriage partner to do for you?

Someone I like, huh...
I'd be happy if they stayed by my side.
That's all I want. Guess I'd be happy if they
smiled after listening to one of my performances.

Alan Stuart

Power Gauge

Wisdom

Power

Stamina

Magic

Charisma

Katarina's adopted brother, taken in by the Claes family due to his high magical aptitude. Considerably handsome, and seen by others as sexy and charming. Although he was originally destined to be abused and lonely, such a fate was averted when he met Katarina and was raised with love by the Claes family. Has grown into a respectable young man, and is still growing.

Likes	Magical studies, snacks (Katarina's influence)
Dislikes	Women who approach him aggressively (during dances where he can't avoid them)
Element	Earth
Special Skills	Supporting Big Sister
Personality	Works hard, can be shy around women

Keith Claes

Q

Is there anything you would like your lover or marriage partner to do for you?

Things I'd want them to do for me?
Perhaps jumping in suddenly when I am in the bath, wearing thin garments and wandering around the house, hugging me suddenly...
Ahem, these activities are all very troubling and I would greatly prefer for her to not do these things.

Power Gauge

Wisdom

Stamina

Power

Charisma

Magic

Character Profiles

Son of Royal Chancellor Ascart. Possesses stunning beauty, like a doll. Loves his younger sister, Sophia, deeply.
Has an alluring charm that does not discriminate between gender or age, and hence is loved by many.
Usually stoic and expressionless, but often smiles happily before Katarina.

Nicol Ascart

Likes	◆ Relaxing times, studies on various subjects
Dislikes	◆ Private conversations (not very good at small talk, or talking at all if they are not his close friends)
Element	◆ Wind
Special Skills	◆ Alluring Charm Aura. Knocks people senseless (he isn't aware of this)

Q

Is there anything you would like your lover or marriage partner to do for you?

I am not very good at small talk, and may be unable to entertain my partner. If possible, I would like her to initiate the conversation. I would also like for her to forgive me even if my responses are bland.

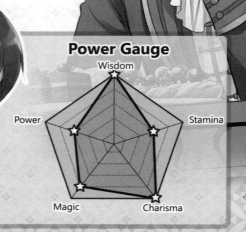

Power Gauge

- Wisdom
- Stamina
- Power
- Charisma
- Magic

Sophia Ascart

Daughter of Royal Chancellor Ascart, and Nicol's younger sister.
A calm and peaceful girl who faced discrimination due to her white hair and red eyes. She loves reading stories, especially romance novels, and ended up bonding with Katarina over them.

Q Is there anything you would like your lover or marriage partner to do for you?

Perhaps whisper to me words of love before a grand field of flowers...? Exchange deep kisses under a night sky full of stars, or to be rescued by them from a terrible fiancé, maybe even save me from an evil mage... etc. etc. (All plot points from romance novels.)

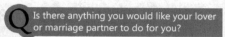

Likes	◆ Novels (especially romance novels)
Dislikes	◆ Crowded places (because of her appearance)
Element	◆ Wind
Special Skills	◆ Fantasizing and daydreaming
Personality	◆ Peaceful and quiet, but became somewhat more outspoken after meeting Katarina

Power Gauge

Mary Hunt

Fourth daughter of Marquis Hunt, and Alan's fiancée.
A likable and beautiful young girl, she is known as the "noble lady amongst noble ladies" in society.
Loves Katarina very much, and would like to bring her to a distant land where she can have her all to herself. (Apparently.)

Q Is there anything you would like your lover or marriage partner to do for you?

Not much that I can think of, if said partner is to be a man. If I really had to come up with something, someone who follows my every command would be best. Someone gullible— I mean, an honest and straightforward person... of course.

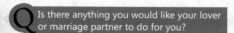

Likes	◆ Plants
Dislikes	◆ Stepmother and stepsisters
Element	◆ Water
Special Skills	◆ Dancing, navigating the politics of noble society
Personality	◆ Although withdrawn and shirking in childhood, now quite headstrong and somewhat conniving

Power Gauge

Maria Campbell

A commoner, but also a rare Wielder of Light—a girl blessed with Light Magic. Originally the protagonist of the game, and a hard worker. Encountered Katarina at the Academy of Magic, and became friends with her after being saved by her many times. Very skilled at baking.

Maria's handmade treats are one of Katarina's favorite foods.

Q Is there anything you would like your lover or marriage partner to do for you?

I would love for them to take me to a wonderful place for a date. And then we would look at the view while eating from a lunchbox that I prepared. Ah... if we are going to have lunch outside, Lady Katarina would be excited if she were invited, too. Back when I was still eating my lunches outside, she did mention that she would love to try my cooking! I'll be sure to invite her if I go on this date.

Power Gauge
Wisdom · Stamina · Charisma · Magic · Power

Likes	Sweets and snacks
Dislikes	Bitter things, spicy things
Element	Light
Special Skills	Baking
Personality	Cheerful and serene, but somewhat simple

Raphael Wolt

A capable and composed young man working for the ministry. Decided to part ways with his old self after crossing paths with Katarina. He now spends his days flailing around to the whims of his free-spirited superior at the ministry.

Q Is there anything you would like your lover or marriage partner to do for you?

It would be nice to come home after a long day at work and have a good meal or a warm bed ready.

Well... I have been sleeping over at the ministry due to the workload as of late, so perhaps I'd never even get to go home to begin with...

Power Gauge
Wisdom · Stamina · Charisma · Magic · Power

Likes	Black tea and snacks that go well with it
Dislikes	Dark, gloomy places
Element	Light
Special Skills	Cleaning up after his carefree boss, brewing good tea
Personality	Serious

Sora

A young man working at the ministry. While his original magical element was fire, it became dark due to certain circumstances.
Born in a slum in a foreign land, he grew up learning how to use and manipulate those around him. Despite his best attempts at communicating his affection for Katarina, it went right over her dense head.

Q Is there anything you would like your lover or marriage partner to do for you?

I've had most things done for me, yeah.
Especially by older ladies... they're pretty amazing.
Eh? It isn't about that? You want from a healthy perspective? Ah, well. Having meals made for me is good. Haven't dated a girl like that before, after all.

Power Gauge

Likes	◆ Gold (money)
Dislikes	◆ Nothing really
Element	◆ Fire
Special Skills	◆ Sweet-talking women
Personality	◆ Positive and forward-looking

Anne Shelley

Katarina's personal maid who has been in her service since she was eight. Although very strict to Katarina on the surface, Katarina is more important to her than anything else in the world. She is always by Katarina's side, no matter what the situation.

Q Is there anything you would like your lover or marriage partner to do for you?

I do not have any family left in the world. If I left this job, I would have nothing else. I hope you can understand that I intend to stay by Lady Katarina's side forever.
However, if someone like that really appears, marriage may not be a bad option, either.

Power Gauge

Likes	◆ Books on Agriculture (influenced by Katarina)
Dislikes	◆ Large fires
Element	◆ None
Special Skills	◆ Predicting Katarina's activities
Personality	◆ Serious, hardworking

The adventures of Katarina, villainess extraordinaire,
and her Catastrophic Bad Ends shall continue...

Hi everyone, I'm Satoru Yamaguchi.

My Next Life as a Villainess has finally reached its fifth volume. This is all thanks to you, the readers. You have all my gratitude!

In this volume, I wrote about some things that happened in the background of previous events. These include the stories that I wrote as extras for the web novel: the ones about the Claes servants, Katarina's parents, her rival, and her friends — Jeord, Alan, Keith, Mary, Sophia, Maria, and of course Nicol with his matchmaking dates. There are a lot of characters to write about!

I hope that you'll read this volume thinking, "Oh, so that's what happened back then!"

Nami Hidaka-sama, other than drawing the usual beautiful illustrations for this volume, has also drawn a wonderful manga, longer than ever before!

I am so grateful to Hidaka-sama for their wonderful work on this manga, as well as those in Volumes 3 and 4. And I can't help but smile any time I read them. And this time it's even longer! Fantastic!

Seeing my characters' stories so beautifully illustrated is an incredible feeling. After seeing them for the first time, I almost passed out! Make sure to read the manga pages!

Thank you so much, Hidaka-sama!

And finally, I also want to thank my editor, as well as all the people that made this book possible.

Thank you from the bottom of my heart.

Satoru Yamaguchi

STOP!

➡️ FORTUNE LOVER MANGA MODE ENGAGED!

➡️ The rest of this book is published in Right-to-Left orientation.

➡️ Please insert Disc 2 or flip the book to the back cover and begin reading again from there.

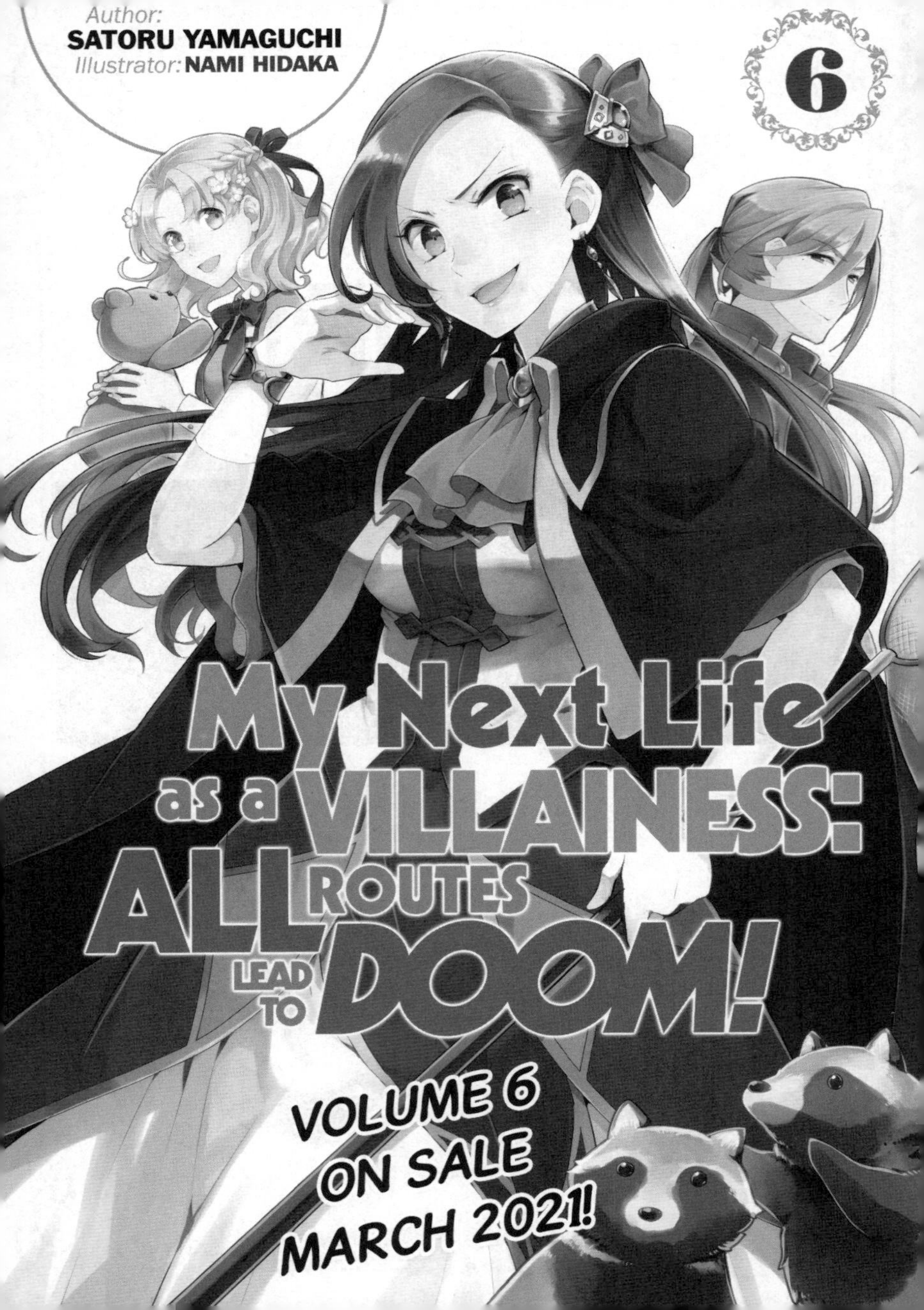
Author:
SATORU YAMAGUCHI
Illustrator: NAMI HIDAKA
6
My Next Life as a VILLAINESS: ALL ROUTES LEAD TO DOOM!
VOLUME 6
ON SALE
MARCH 2021!

OH, DEAR. BAD ENDS
AWAIT THOSE WHO
DON'T LISTEN.

IT SSSSSSSSSSSSSSSSSSAID
TO FLIP THE BOOK OVER...

STOP!

➡️ FORTUNE LOVER NOVEL MODE ENGAGED!

➡️ The rest of this book is published in Left-to-Right orientation.

➡️ Please insert Disc 1 or flip the book to the front cover and begin reading again from there.

Angels

Reinforcements 3
Maria and Raphael
Main Role: Harmless at a glance,
but are actually involved in an operation to
separate Katarina from Prince Jeord.

And of
course,
the force
opposing
them...

PRINCE JEORD

Katarina's fiancé. Has a sadistic streak.
Sole member of the "Katarina shall
become my Queen" faction.

Ha
ha
ha!

Fu-
haha-
haha!

And
this is
the dark
horse
worth
keeping
an eye
on.

The title
of fiancé is
not just for
show! Just
one of him is
more than
enough! The
indomitable
Prince Jeord!

The people around Katarina Claes...

Are largely separated into two factions.

About the Factions

Main Members
Keith (Adopted Brother) and Madame Claes (Mother)
Main Role:
Attempt to make Prince Jeord cancel his engagement with Katarina. Work hard daily. Not afraid to use force.

The "Katarina (Big Sister) cannot possibly fulfill the duties of Queen" faction

Reinforcements 2
Nicol and Sophia
Main Role: Become familiar with Katarina's preferences. Secretly aiming for Katarina herself.

Reinforcements 1
Prince Alan and Mary
Main Role:
Prevent Katarina from approaching Prince Jeord, and vice versa.

IT IS SO DIFFICULT TO DECIDE...

OR PERHAPS A BIRD, OR FISH. I'D SWIM IN THE SEA OR FLY IN THE SKY!

ムキ FLEX

ムキ FLEX

I THINK I WOULD LIKE TO TRY BEING A STRONG MAN SO I COULD CARRY HEAVY THINGS!

Maria Campbell

AH, BUT I SUPPOSE I COULD DO THAT WITHOUT GETTING REINCARNATED...

SOMEONE WITH A JOB THAT IS REGULATED BY PROPER LABOR STANDARDS...

REINCARNA-TION, YOU SAY...

YES, OF COURSE.

Raphael Wolt

I'D PLAY AROUND AS MUCH AS I WANT!

A SUPER RICH GUY!

Sora

3 — 33 — ♪
LA-DI-DA

E'S ROOM

Yet another rival appears ...!

PERHAPS A PERSON THAT COULD BE CLOSE TO LADY KATARINA.

WELL THEN, THAT IS ALL FOR TODAY.

OH, ME? I HAVE NO PARTICULAR OPINION.

THANK YOU VERY MUCH.

3 3 3
LA-DI-DA

3 — 3—

LA-DI-DA

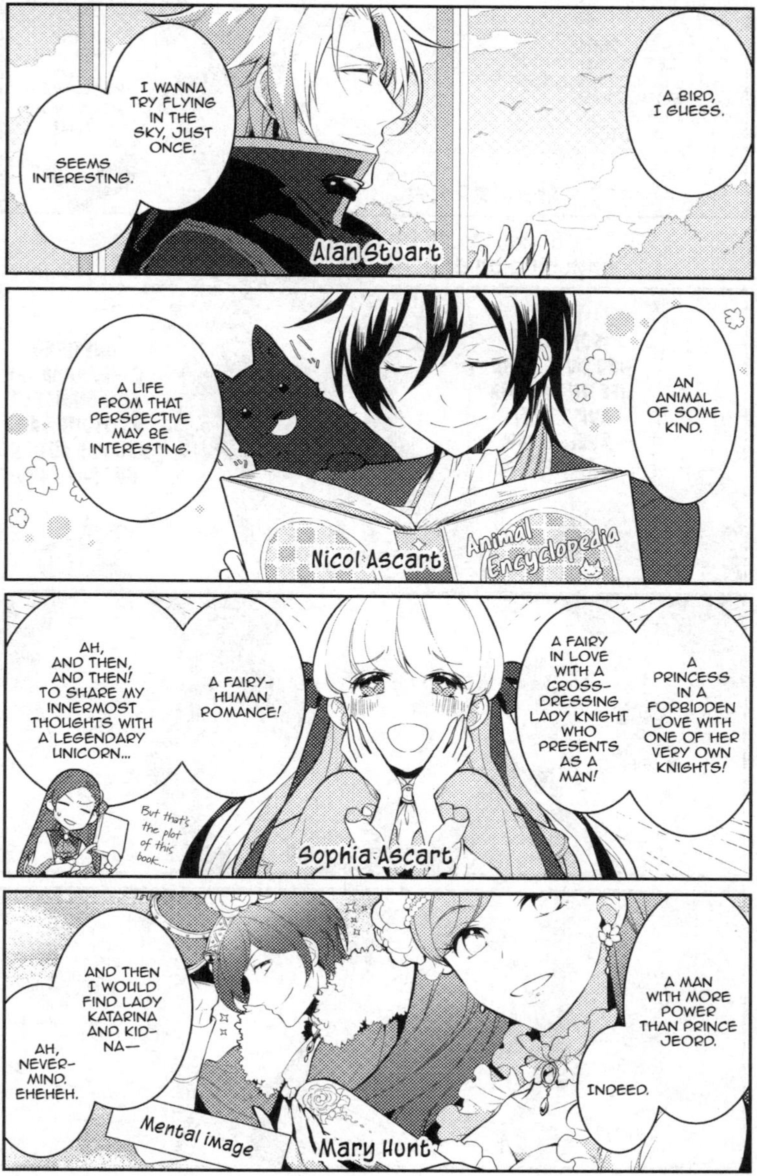
A BIRD, I GUESS.
I WANNA TRY FLYING IN THE SKY, JUST ONCE.
SEEMS INTERESTING.
Alan Stuart
AN ANIMAL OF SOME KIND.
A LIFE FROM THAT PERSPECTIVE MAY BE INTERESTING.
Animal Encyclopedia
Nicol Ascart
A PRINCESS IN A FORBIDDEN LOVE WITH ONE OF HER VERY OWN KNIGHTS!
A FAIRY IN LOVE WITH A CROSS-DRESSING LADY KNIGHT WHO PRESENTS AS A MAN!
A FAIRY-HUMAN ROMANCE!
AH, AND THEN, AND THEN! TO SHARE MY INNERMOST THOUGHTS WITH A LEGENDARY UNICORN...
But that's the plot of this book...
Sophia Ascart
A MAN WITH MORE POWER THAN PRINCE JEORD.
INDEED.
AND THEN I WOULD FIND LADY KATARINA AND KID-NA—
AH, NEVER-MIND. EHEHEH.
Mental image
Mary Hunt

WELL THEN. LET US ASK EVERYONE SOME QUESTIONS TODAY AS WELL.

GREETINGS. IT IS I, ANNE SHELLEY, LADY KATARINA'S PERSONAL MAID.

Anne's Room

If you could be reincarnated as anything or anyone, what would you be?

Game? Anime...?

SOMEONE WHO LIVES A FUN LIFE WITH MANGA AND ANIME! A FULFILLING 2D LIFE!

ANYTHING OTHER THAN THE ANTAGONIST OF AN OTOME GAME WHO HAS NOTHING BUT BAD ENDS!

Katarina Claes

IF THAT CAME TO PASS...

MANY THINGS WOULD BECOME EASIER.

SOMEONE WHO HAS MORE FREEDOM TO ROAM, AND IS FREE OF ANY SOCIAL STATIONS...

Shiver

Chuckle

?

shiver

?

Jeord Stuart

PERHAPS IT IS DUE TO BIG SISTER'S INFLUENCE, BUT I KNOW LITTLE OF HOW NORMAL GIRLS FEEL...

I WOULDN'T MIND TRYING OUT BEING A GIRL...

Big sister!

Mental image

Hmm...

Keith Claes

GUESS I'VE NEVER BEEN ON A HEALTHY DATE.

BUT IF YOU NEED AN ANSWER...

I'VE PLAYED THE FIELD FOR A LONG TIME.

IT'S PART OF MY JOB TO SWEET-TALK WOMEN, SO I'VE DONE IT ALL...

Swish

DIRTY DETAILS?

SHOULD I GET INTO THE...

SMIRK

SILENCE...

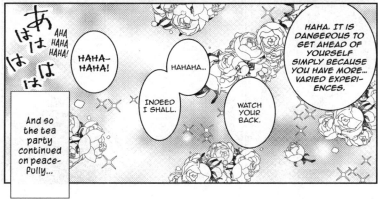

AHA HAHA HAHA!

HAHA-HAHA!

HAHAHA...

HAHA. IT IS DANGEROUS TO GET AHEAD OF YOURSELF SIMPLY BECAUSE YOU HAVE MORE... VARIED EXPERI-ENCES.

INDEED I SHALL.

WATCH YOUR BACK.

And so the tea party continued on peace-fully...

I HAVE NOTICED THAT THIS IS OFTEN NOT THE CASE.

MOST WOULD CONSIDER THAT NORMAL FOR A COUPLE. HOWEVER...

I WOULD SEND HER FLOWERS AND WE WOULD SHARE MEALS TOGETHER.

I WOULD TREAT HER LOVINGLY EVERY DAY, AS MY FATHER DOES WITH MY MOTHER.

SOME FRESH, DELICIOUS RED TEA WOULD BE NICE.

AHH, BUT RECENTLY...

I LOVE BREWING TEA, SO I'D MAKE SOME TEA FOR HER.

Hmm...

I'M LAST, HUH.

I MEAN...

AREN'T YOU THE ONE WHO NEEDS A MASSAGE...?

AND I HAVE BECOME QUITE GOOD AT IT...

I HAVE BEEN GIVING TIRED COLLEAGUES OF MINE MASSAGES...

Haha... Sigh...

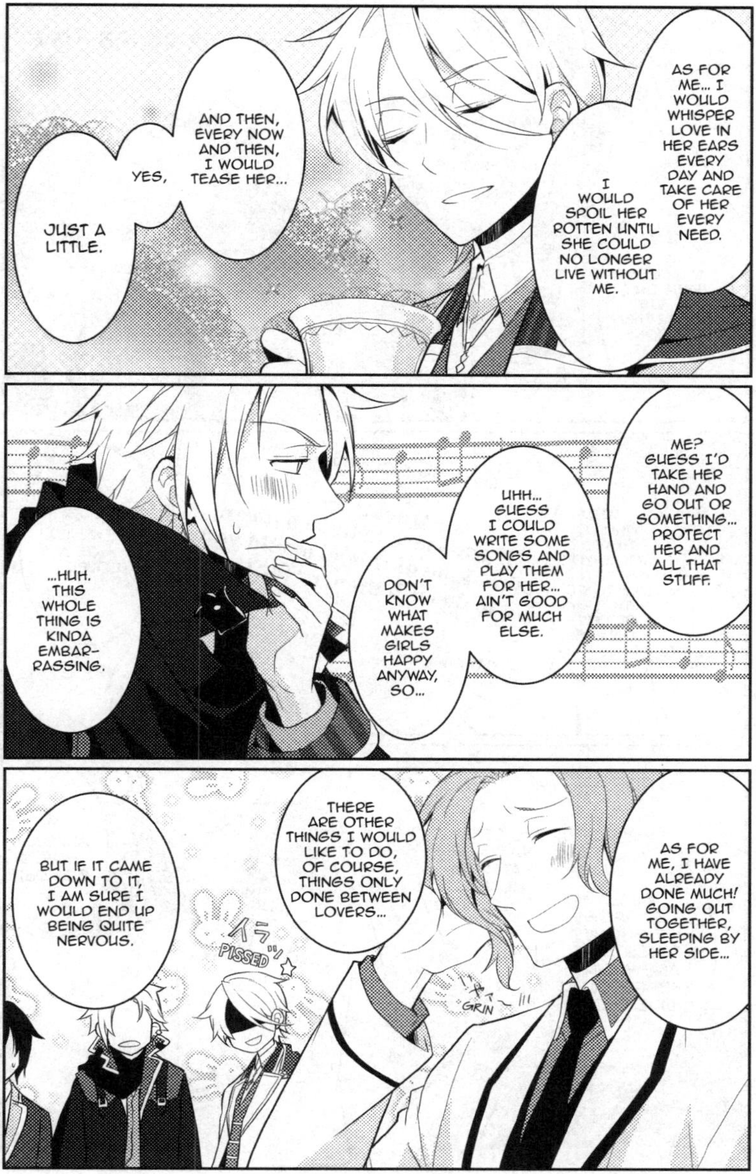
AS FOR ME... I WOULD WHISPER LOVE IN HER EARS EVERY DAY AND TAKE CARE OF HER EVERY NEED.
I WOULD SPOIL HER ROTTEN UNTIL SHE COULD NO LONGER LIVE WITHOUT ME.
AND THEN, EVERY NOW AND THEN, I WOULD TEASE HER...
YES,
JUST A LITTLE.
ME? GUESS I'D TAKE HER HAND AND GO OUT OR SOMETHING... PROTECT HER AND ALL THAT STUFF.
UHH... GUESS I COULD WRITE SOME SONGS AND PLAY THEM FOR HER... AIN'T GOOD FOR MUCH ELSE.
DON'T KNOW WHAT MAKES GIRLS HAPPY ANYWAY, SO...
...HUH. THIS WHOLE THING IS KINDA EMBARRASSING.
AS FOR ME, I HAVE ALREADY DONE MUCH! GOING OUT TOGETHER, SLEEPING BY HER SIDE...
THERE ARE OTHER THINGS I WOULD LIKE TO DO, OF COURSE, THINGS ONLY DONE BETWEEN LOVERS...
GRIN
イラッ
PISSED
BUT IF IT CAME DOWN TO IT, I AM SURE I WOULD END UP BEING QUITE NERVOUS.

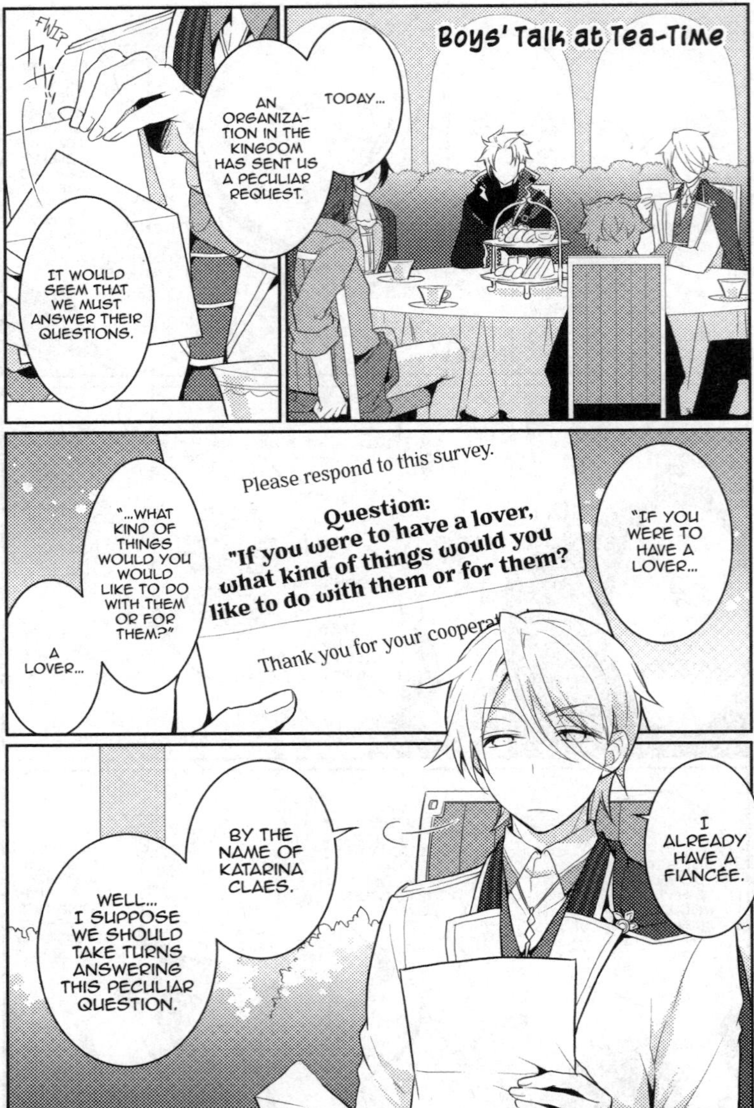
Boys' Talk at Tea-Time
TODAY... AN ORGANIZATION IN THE KINGDOM HAS SENT US A PECULIAR REQUEST.
FWIP
IT WOULD SEEM THAT WE MUST ANSWER THEIR QUESTIONS.
"IF YOU WERE TO HAVE A LOVER...
Please respond to this survey.
Question:
"If you were to have a lover, what kind of things would you like to do with them or for them?
Thank you for your cooperat
"...WHAT KIND OF THINGS WOULD YOU WOULD LIKE TO DO WITH THEM OR FOR THEM?"
A LOVER...
I ALREADY HAVE A FIANCÉE.
BY THE NAME OF KATARINA CLAES.
WELL... I SUPPOSE WE SHOULD TAKE TURNS ANSWERING THIS PECULIAR QUESTION.

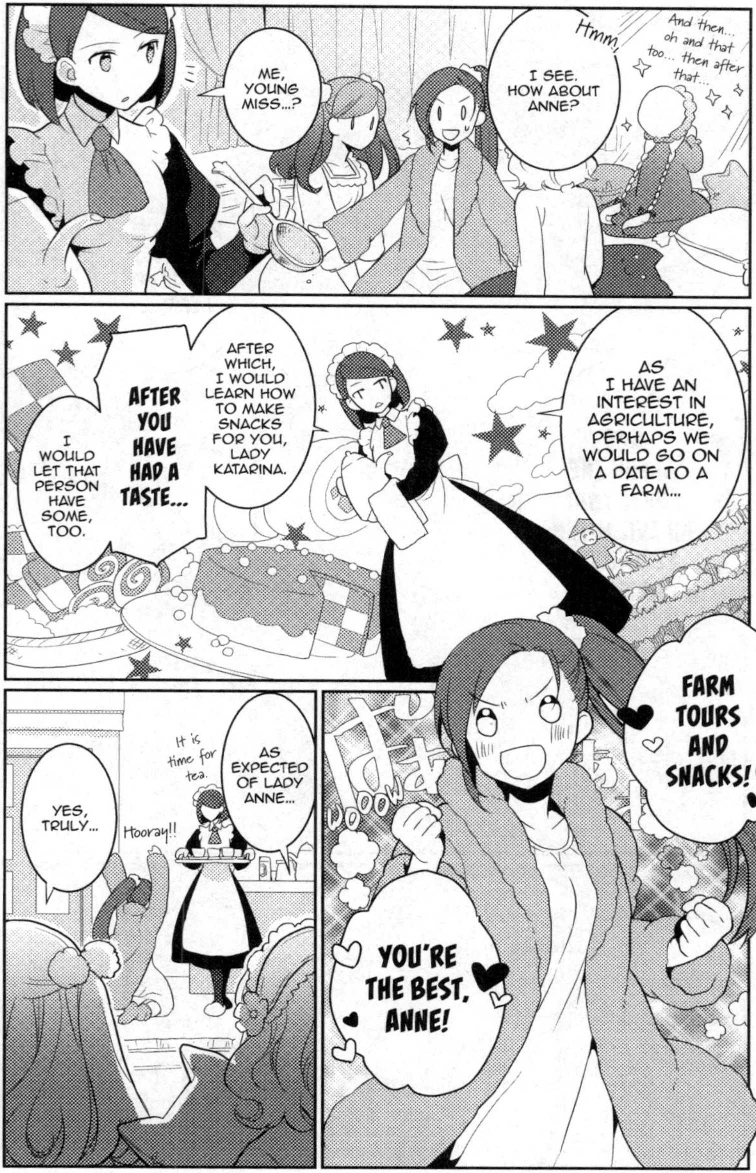
And then... oh and that too... then after that...
Hmm!
I SEE. HOW ABOUT ANNE?
ME, YOUNG MISS...?
AS I HAVE AN INTEREST IN AGRICULTURE, PERHAPS WE WOULD GO ON A DATE TO A FARM...
AFTER WHICH, I WOULD LEARN HOW TO MAKE SNACKS FOR YOU, LADY KATARINA.
AFTER YOU HAVE HAD A TASTE...
I WOULD LET THAT PERSON HAVE SOME, TOO.
FARM TOURS AND SNACKS!
YOU'RE THE BEST, ANNE!
AS EXPECTED OF LADY ANNE...
It is time for tea.
Hooray!!
YES, TRULY...

WE WILL JOIN HANDS AND FIGHT FOR THE FUTURE OF THE KINGDOM!

AND I SHALL DISPEL THE DARKNESS DEEP IN HIS HEART...

AND BREAK THE CURSE THAT AN EVIL WITCH PLACED ON HIM...!

WELL, I SUPPOSE THAT WOULD BE COMMONPLACE IN A NOVEL...?

Whisper

MUNDANE...?

I've read that one before....

YEP, FROM A ROMANCE NOVEL.

Mutter

Mutter

UM, LADY KATARINA, ISN'T THIS...

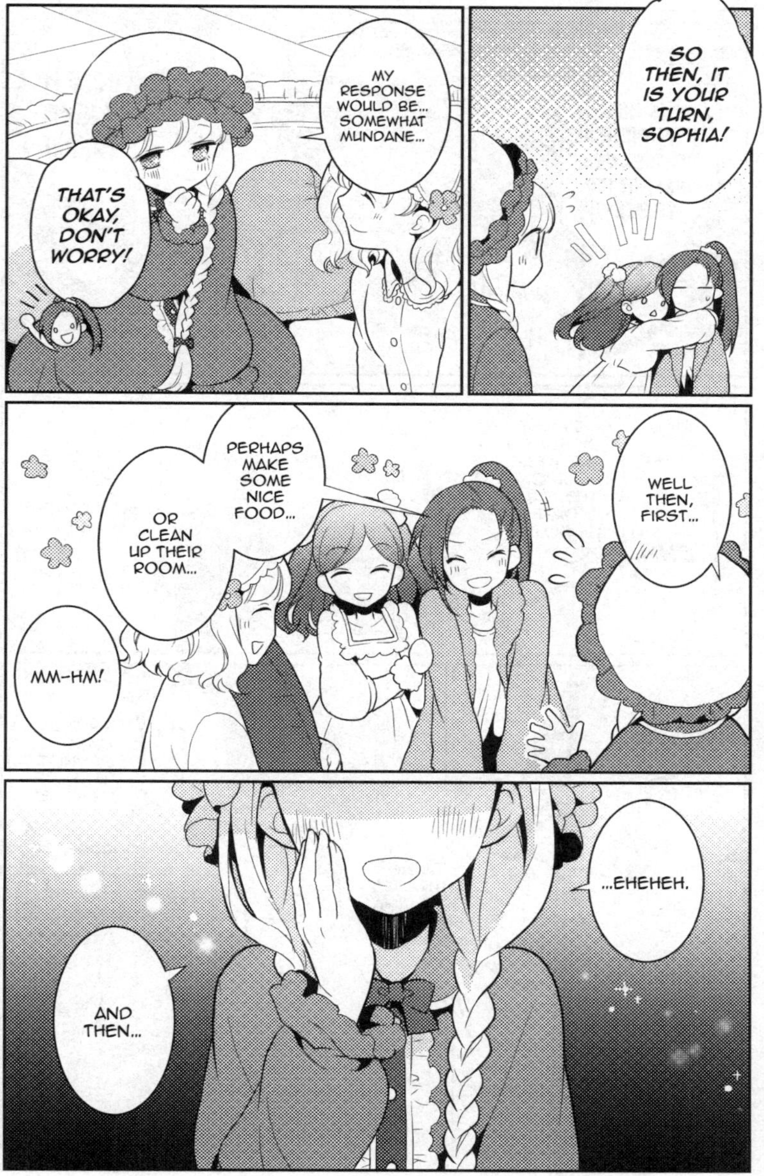
SO THEN, IT IS YOUR TURN, SOPHIA!
MY RESPONSE WOULD BE... SOMEWHAT MUNDANE...
THAT'S OKAY, DON'T WORRY!
WELL THEN, FIRST...
PERHAPS MAKE SOME NICE FOOD...
OR CLEAN UP THEIR ROOM...
MM-HM!
...EHEHEH.
AND THEN...

IS THIS HYPOTHETICAL PARTNER ONLY RESTRICTED TO MEN?!

HOLD IT RIGHT THERE!

WHOA!

I JUST ASSUMED WE WERE ALL ON THE SAME PAGE, SO...

EHH...

Hmph...

WELL, I GUESS WE DIDN'T REALLY SPECIFY THE GENDER...

FLOP

IN THAT CASE, I CANNOT THINK OF ANYONE!

BEING WITH LADY KATARINA LIKE THIS...

IS WHAT MAKES ME HAPPY.

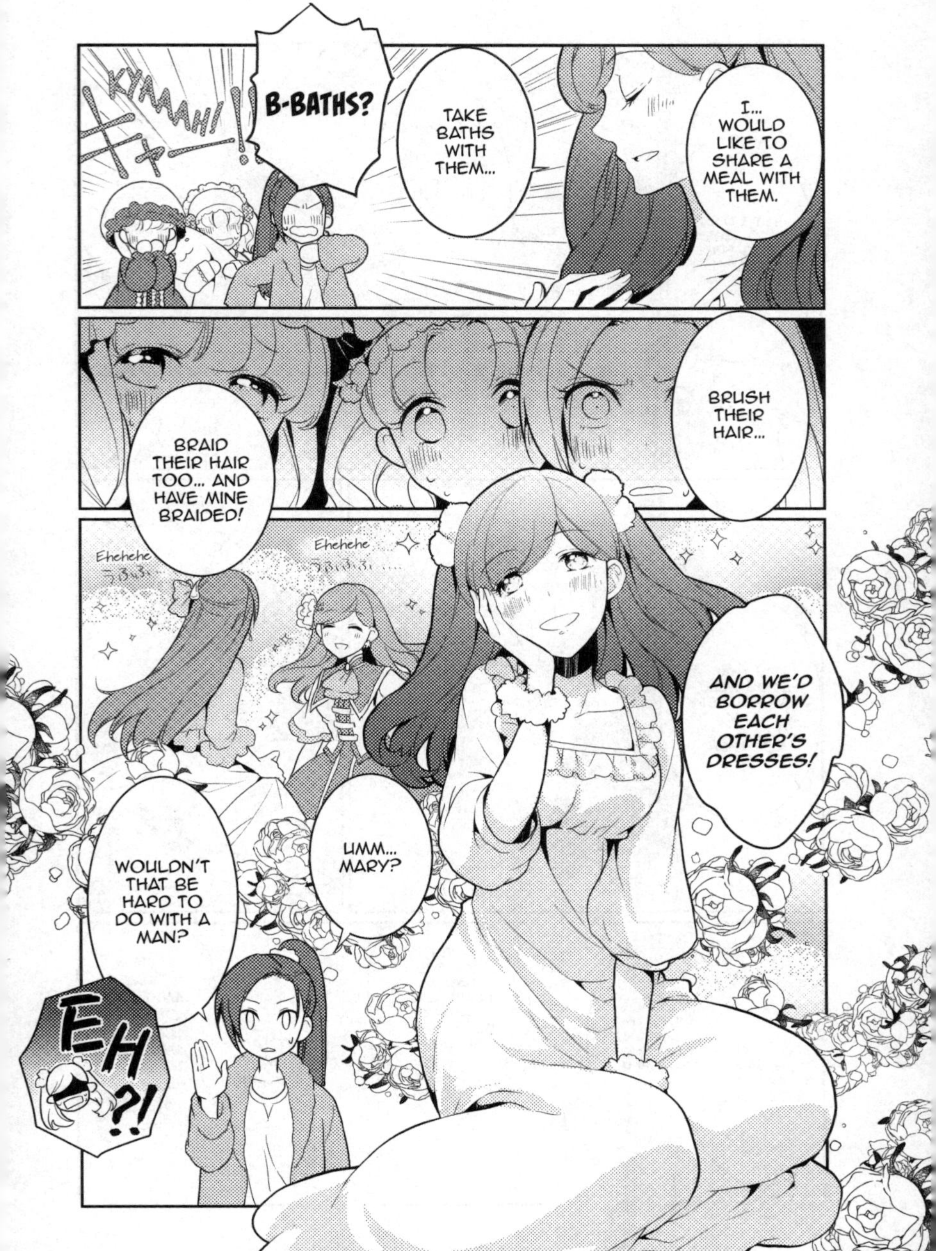
I... WOULD LIKE TO SHARE A MEAL WITH THEM.
TAKE BATHS WITH THEM...
B-BATHS?
KYAAAH!!
BRUSH THEIR HAIR...
BRAID THEIR HAIR TOO... AND HAVE MINE BRAIDED!
AND WE'D BORROW EACH OTHER'S DRESSES!
Ehehehe
Ehehehe
UMM... MARY?
WOULDN'T THAT BE HARD TO DO WITH A MAN?
EH?!

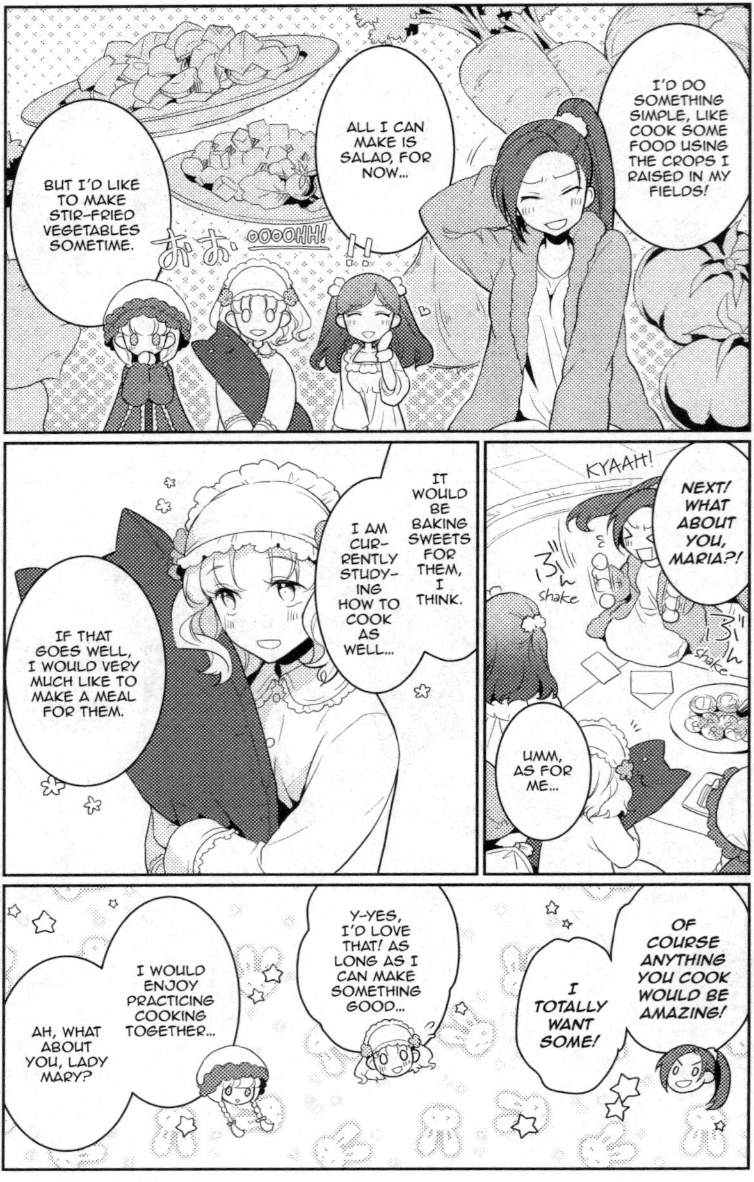
I'D DO SOMETHING SIMPLE, LIKE COOK SOME FOOD USING THE CROPS I RAISED IN MY FIELDS!
ALL I CAN MAKE IS SALAD, FOR NOW...
BUT I'D LIKE TO MAKE STIR-FRIED VEGETABLES SOMETIME.
おお OOOOHH!
!!
KYAAH!
NEXT! WHAT ABOUT YOU, MARIA?!
ぶん shake
ぶん shake
UMM, AS FOR ME...
IT WOULD BE BAKING SWEETS FOR THEM, I THINK.
I AM CURRENTLY STUDYING HOW TO COOK AS WELL...
IF THAT GOES WELL, I WOULD VERY MUCH LIKE TO MAKE A MEAL FOR THEM.
OF COURSE ANYTHING YOU COOK WOULD BE AMAZING!
I TOTALLY WANT SOME!
Y-YES, I'D LOVE THAT! AS LONG AS I CAN MAKE SOMETHING GOOD...
I WOULD ENJOY PRACTICING COOKING TOGETHER...
AH, WHAT ABOUT YOU, LADY MARY?

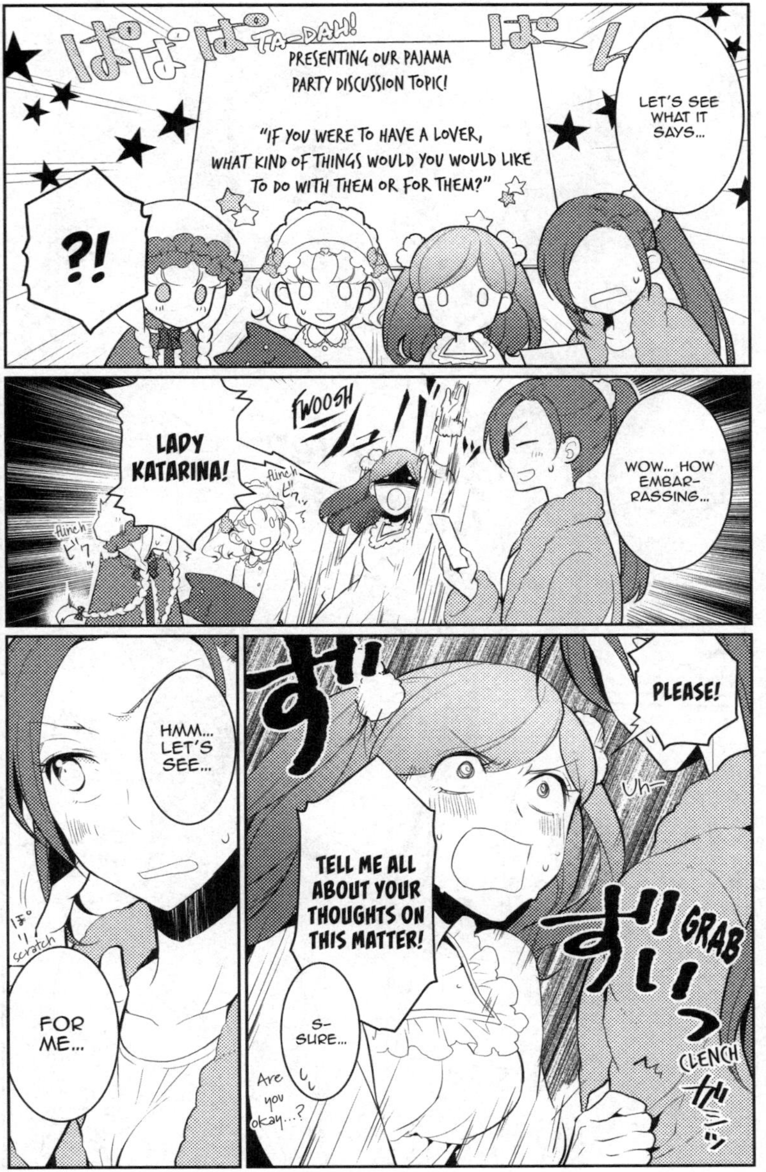
ぱぱぱ
TA-DAH!
ぱーん
LET'S SEE WHAT IT SAYS...
PRESENTING OUR PAJAMA PARTY DISCUSSION TOPIC!
"IF YOU WERE TO HAVE A LOVER, WHAT KIND OF THINGS WOULD YOU WOULD LIKE TO DO WITH THEM OR FOR THEM?"
?!
WOW... HOW EMBARRASSING...
FWOOSH
flinch
LADY KATARINA!
flinch
PLEASE!
TELL ME ALL ABOUT YOUR THOUGHTS ON THIS MATTER!
GRAB
CLENCH
S-SURE...
Are you okay...?
HMM... LET'S SEE...
scratch
FOR ME...

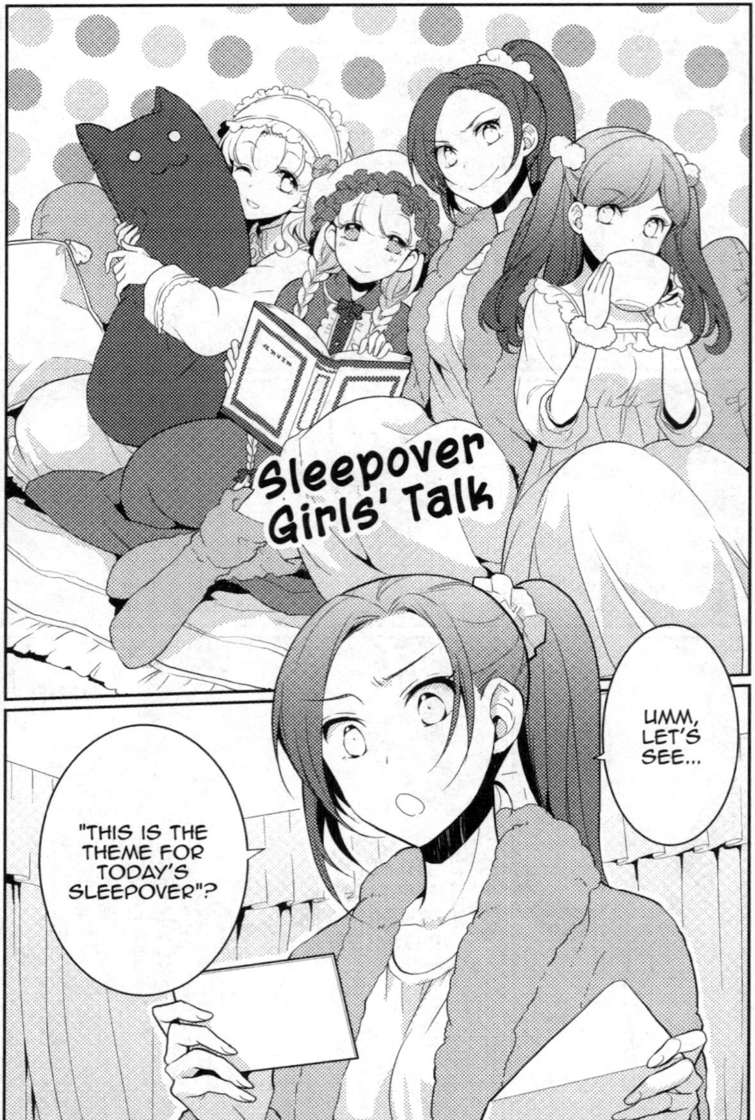
Sleepover Girls' Talk
UMM, LET'S SEE...
"THIS IS THE THEME FOR TODAY'S SLEEPOVER"?

THEY CAME OUT REALLY WELL, SO WE THOUGHT WE'D SHARE THEM WITH YOU BOTH!

YES! I GAVE THEM MY ALL!

EHEH!

Maria-Made

TWINKLE

...I SEE.

THANK YOU FOR THE THOUGHT... KATARINA...

Perhaps now, you may understand...

GLOOM

Katarina-Made

Although these cookies were born of the same dough, those that Big Sister made had an otherworldly taste...

Perhaps this is a talent... or a curse?

To this day, the truth remains a mystery...

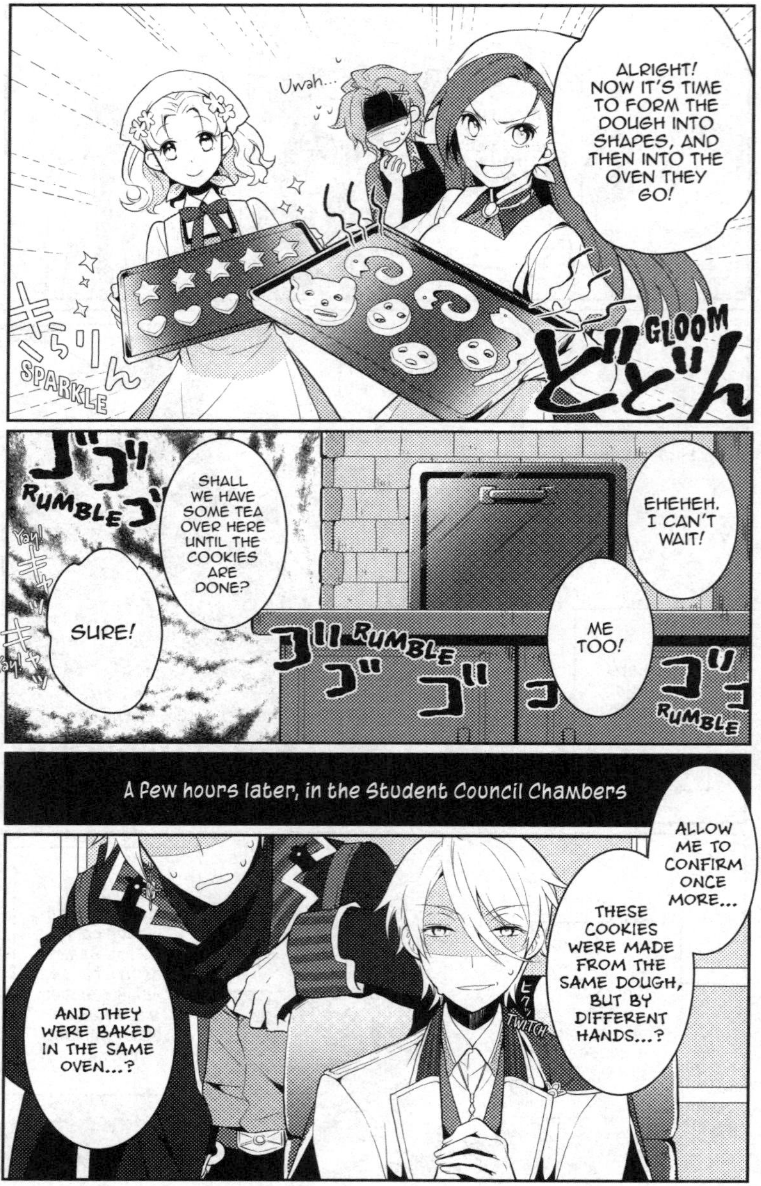
ALRIGHT! NOW IT'S TIME TO FORM THE DOUGH INTO SHAPES, AND THEN INTO THE OVEN THEY GO!
Uwah...
GLOOM
どどん
きらりん
SPARKLE
EHEHEH. I CAN'T WAIT!
ME TOO!
SHALL WE HAVE SOME TEA OVER HERE UNTIL THE COOKIES ARE DONE?
SURE!
Yay!
キャッ
キャッ
Yay!
ゴゴゴ
RUMBLE
RUMBLE
RUMBLE
A few hours later, in the Student Council Chambers
ALLOW ME TO CONFIRM ONCE MORE...
THESE COOKIES WERE MADE FROM THE SAME DOUGH, BUT BY DIFFERENT HANDS...?
ビクッ
TWITCH
AND THEY WERE BAKED IN THE SAME OVEN...?

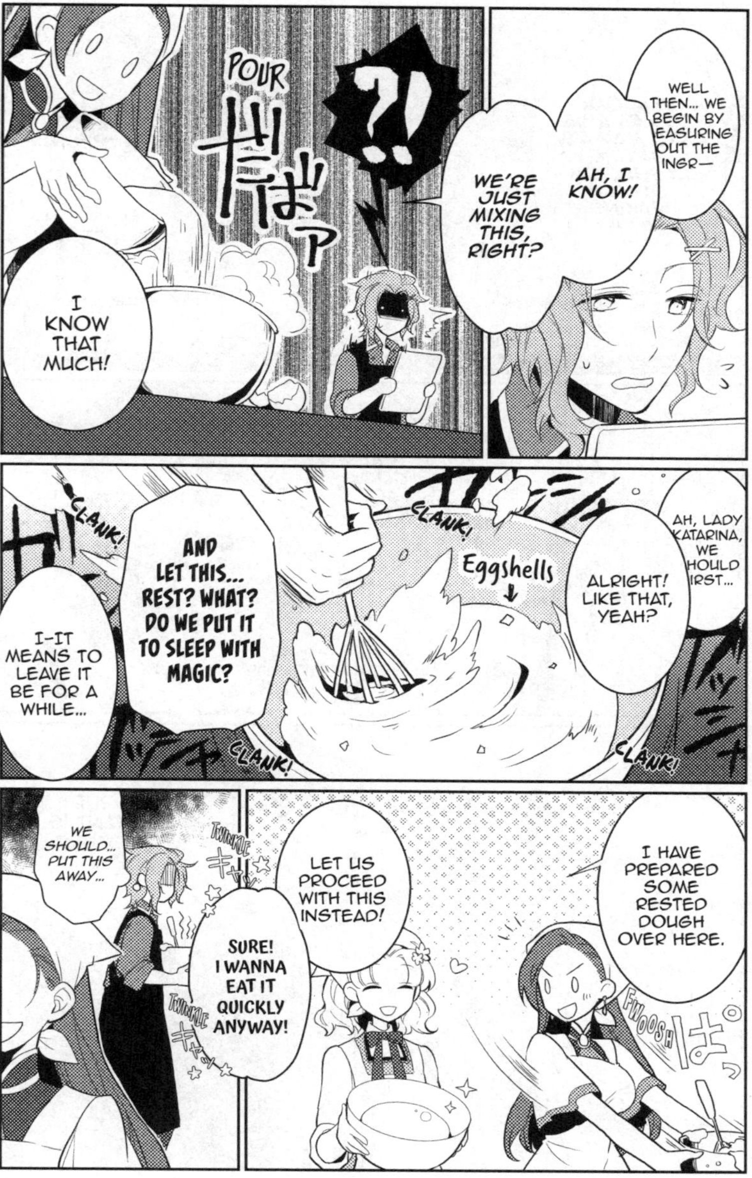
WELL THEN... WE BEGIN BY EASURING OUT THE INGR—
AH, I KNOW!
WE'RE JUST MIXING THIS, RIGHT?
?!
POUR
だばァ
I KNOW THAT MUCH!
AH, LADY ATARINA, WE SHOULD IRST...
ALRIGHT! LIKE THAT, YEAH?
CLANK!
Eggshells
CLANK!
CLANK!
CLANK!
AND LET THIS... REST? WHAT? DO WE PUT IT TO SLEEP WITH MAGIC?
I-IT MEANS TO LEAVE IT BE FOR A WHILE...
I HAVE PREPARED SOME RESTED DOUGH OVER HERE.
FWOOSH はっ
LET US PROCEED WITH THIS INSTEAD!
SURE! I WANNA EAT IT QUICKLY ANYWAY!
TWINKLE キャッ
TWINKLE キャッ
WE SHOULD... PUT THIS AWAY...

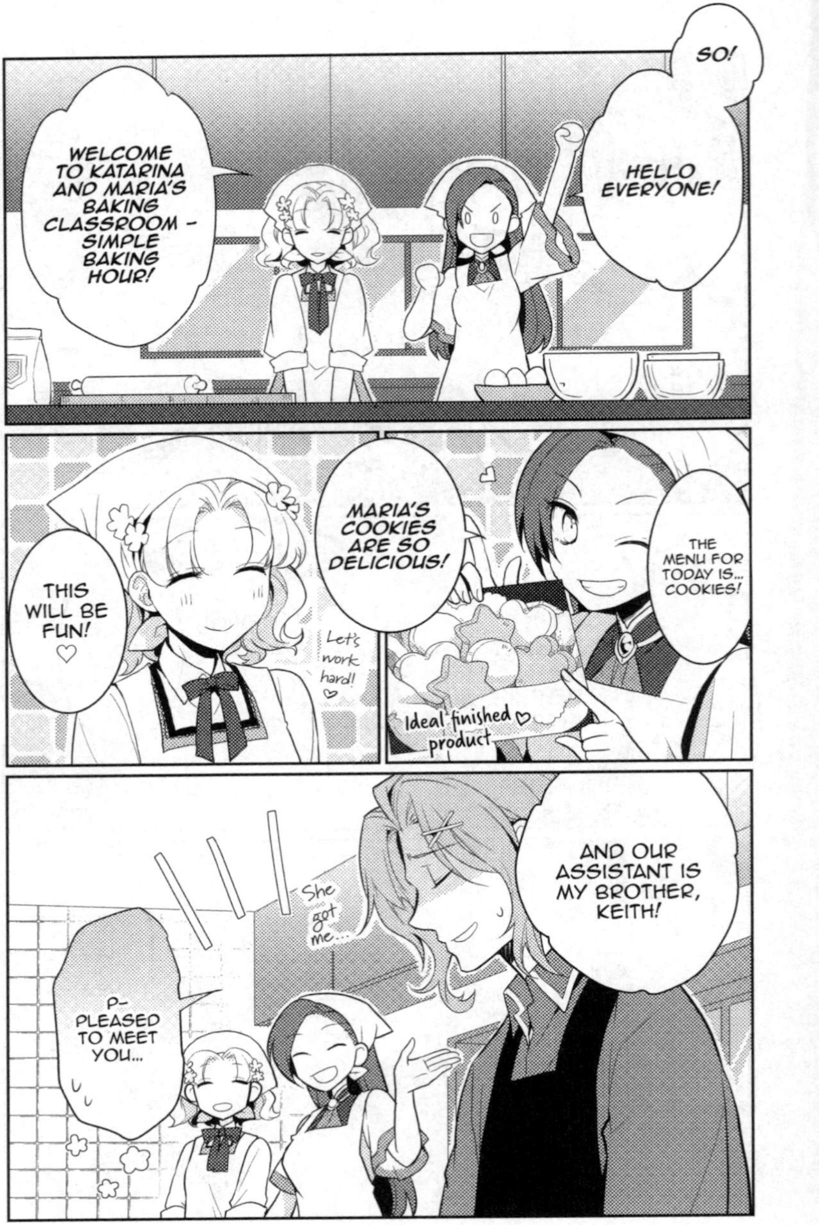
SO!
HELLO EVERYONE!
WELCOME TO KATARINA AND MARIA'S BAKING CLASSROOM - SIMPLE BAKING HOUR!
THE MENU FOR TODAY IS... COOKIES!
Ideal finished product ♡
MARIA'S COOKIES ARE SO DELICIOUS!
THIS WILL BE FUN! ♡
Let's work hard! ♡
AND OUR ASSISTANT IS MY BROTHER, KEITH!
She got me...
P-PLEASED TO MEET YOU...

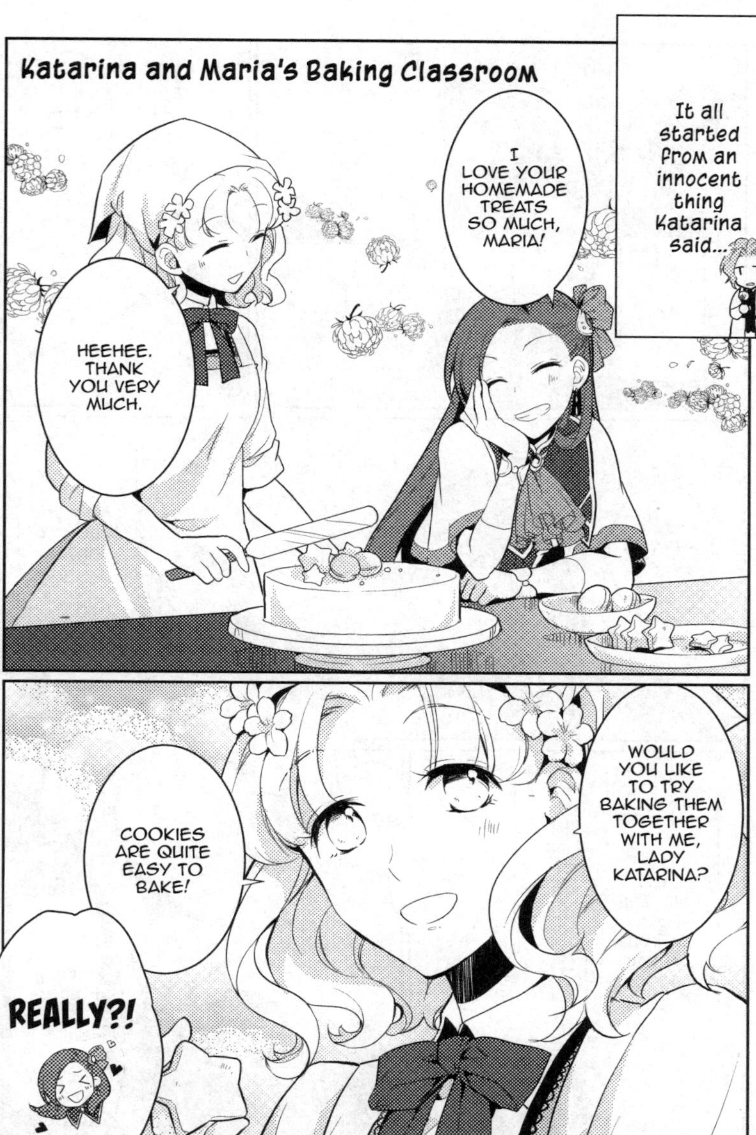
Katarina and Maria's Baking Classroom
It all started from an innocent thing Katarina said...
I LOVE YOUR HOMEMADE TREATS SO MUCH, MARIA!
HEEHEE. THANK YOU VERY MUCH.
WOULD YOU LIKE TO TRY BAKING THEM TOGETHER WITH ME, LADY KATARINA?
COOKIES ARE QUITE EASY TO BAKE!
REALLY?!

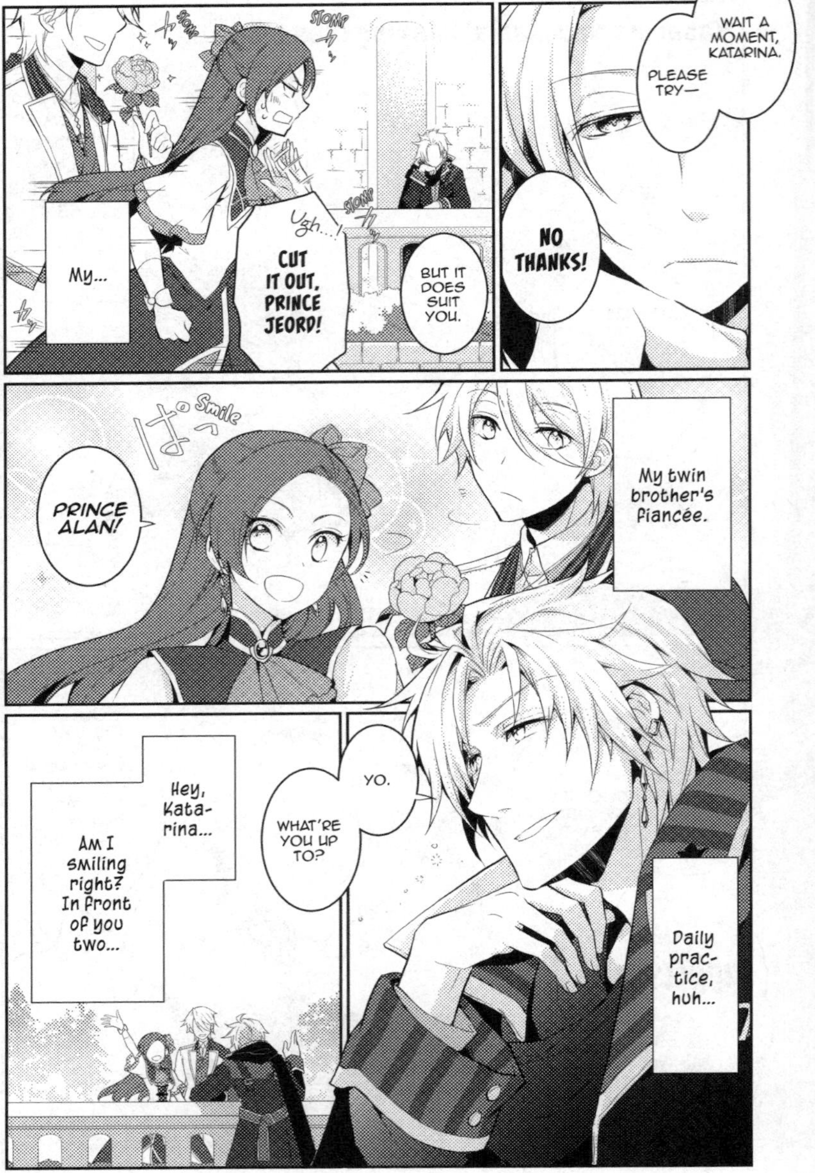
WAIT A MOMENT, KATARINA.
PLEASE TRY—
NO THANKS!
STOMP
STOMP
STOMP
Ugh...!
CUT IT OUT, PRINCE JEORD!
BUT IT DOES SUIT YOU.
My...
Smile
PRINCE ALAN!
My twin brother's fiancée.
YO.
WHAT'RE YOU UP TO?
Daily prac-tice, huh...
Hey, Kata-rina...
Am I smiling right? In front of you two...

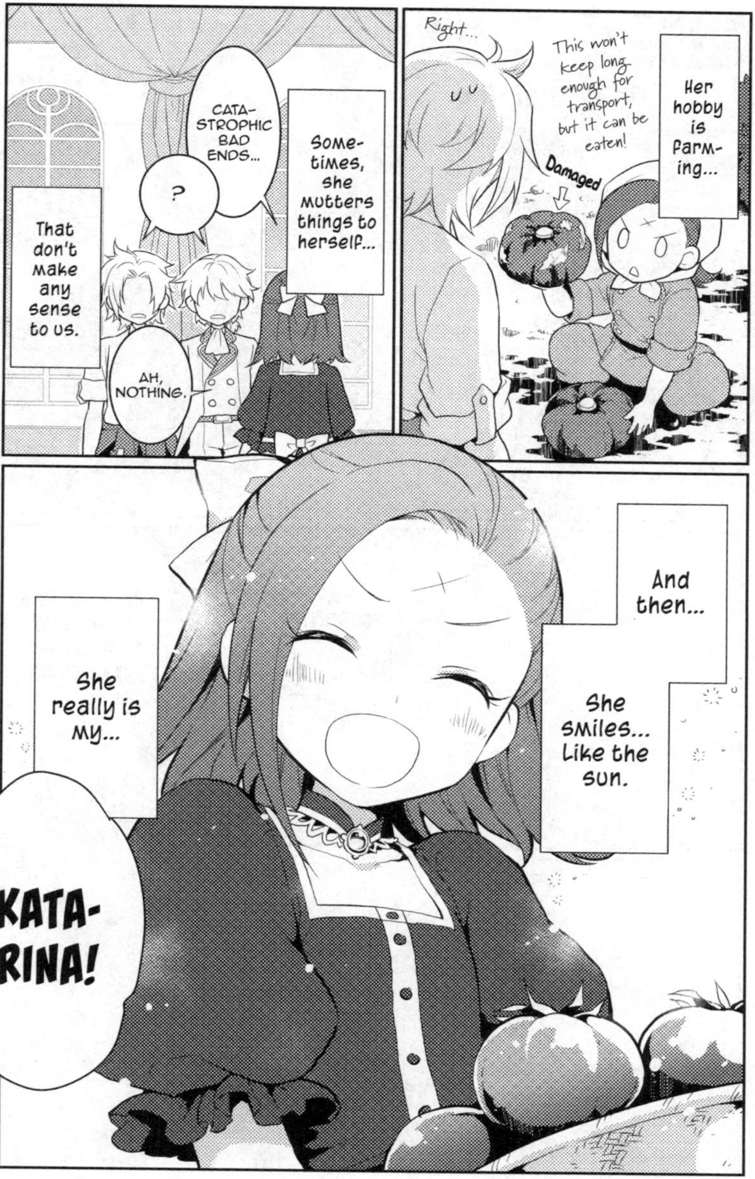
Her hobby is farming...
This won't keep long enough for transport, but it can be eaten!
Damaged
Right...
Sometimes, she mutters things to herself...
CATASTROPHIC BAD ENDS...
?
AH, NOTHING.
That don't make any sense to us.
And then...
She smiles... Like the sun.
She really is my...
KATARINA!

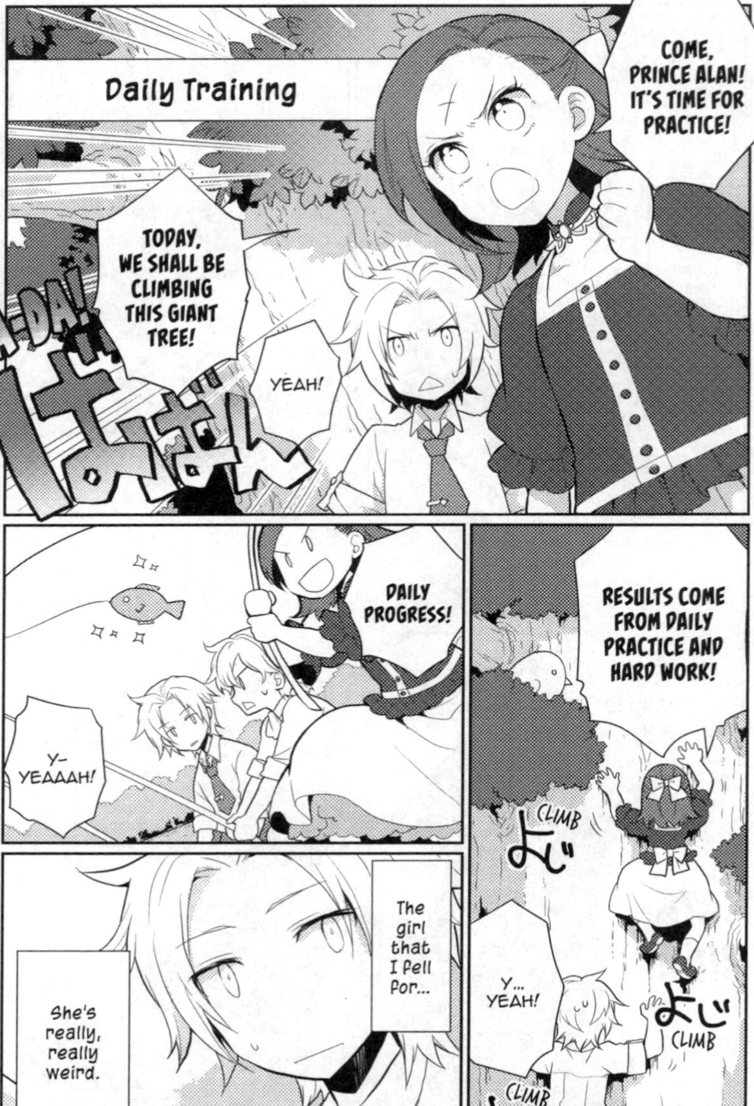

Daily Training
COME, PRINCE ALAN! IT'S TIME FOR PRACTICE!
TODAY, WE SHALL BE CLIMBING THIS GIANT TREE!
TA-DA!!
ばばん
YEAH!
RESULTS COME FROM DAILY PRACTICE AND HARD WORK!
CLIMB
よじ
Y... YEAH!
よじ
CLIMB
CLIMB
よじ
DAILY PROGRESS!
Y-YEAAAH!
The girl that I fell for...
She's really, really weird.

• For your consideration •
These depictions of Katarina contain stories from both her past and present, as well as people she has met. These snippets will contain stories from the first volume as well. Lastly, this is a work of fiction. Any resemblance to any individuals, organizations, incidents, or games is purely coincidental.

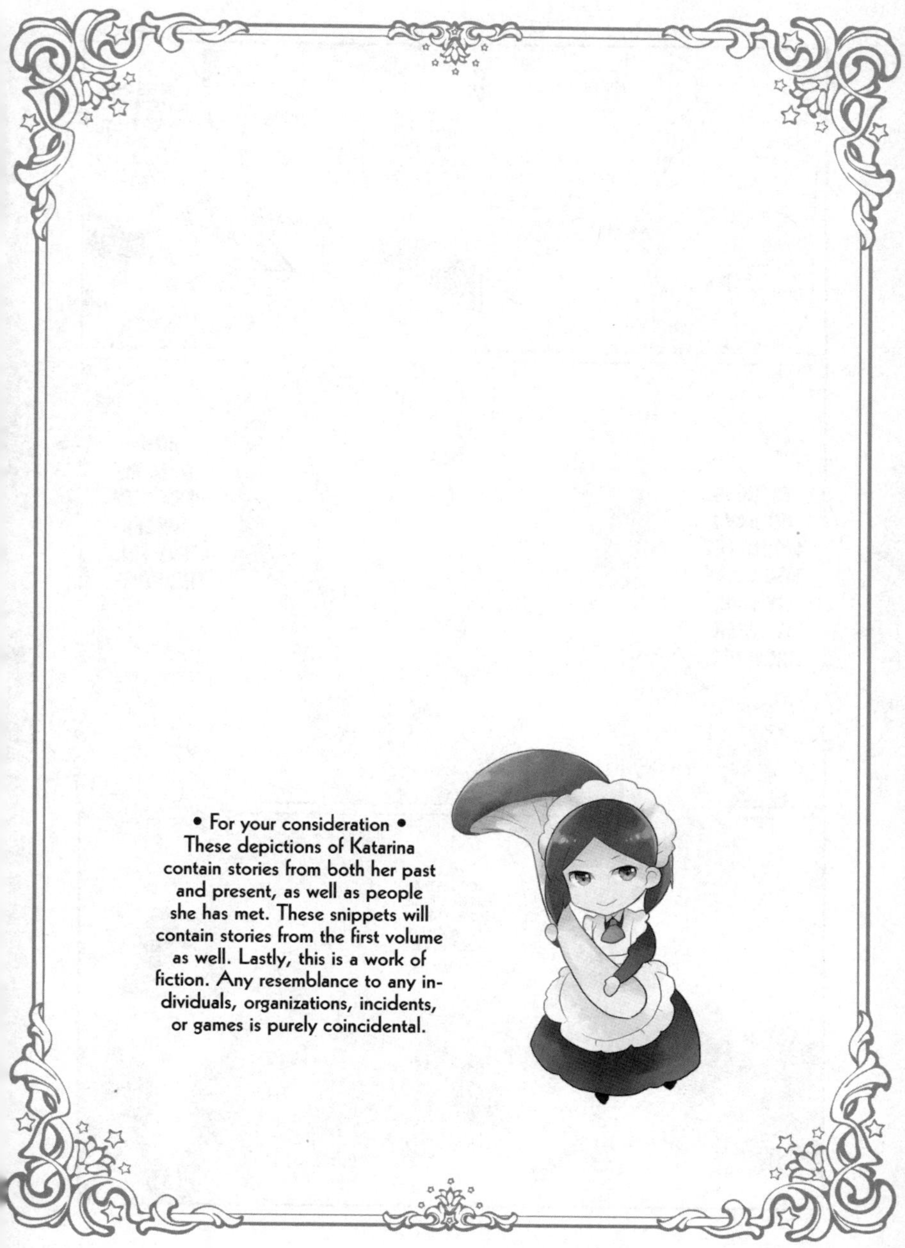

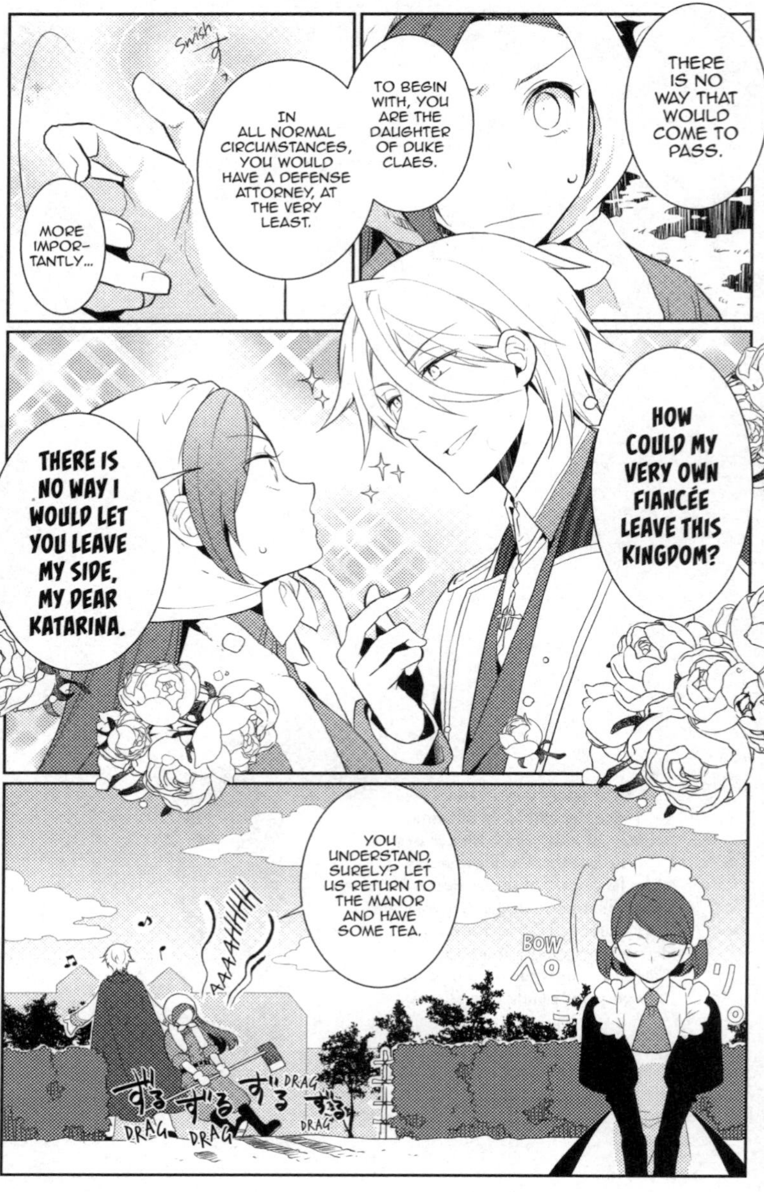
THERE IS NO WAY THAT WOULD COME TO PASS.
TO BEGIN WITH, YOU ARE THE DAUGHTER OF DUKE CLAES.
IN ALL NORMAL CIRCUMSTANCES, YOU WOULD HAVE A DEFENSE ATTORNEY, AT THE VERY LEAST.
Swish
MORE IMPORTANTLY...
HOW COULD MY VERY OWN FIANCÉE LEAVE THIS KINGDOM?
THERE IS NO WAY I WOULD LET YOU LEAVE MY SIDE, MY DEAR KATARINA.
BOW
YOU UNDERSTAND, SURELY? LET US RETURN TO THE MANOR AND HAVE SOME TEA.
AAAAHHHH
DRAG DRAG DRAG DRAG

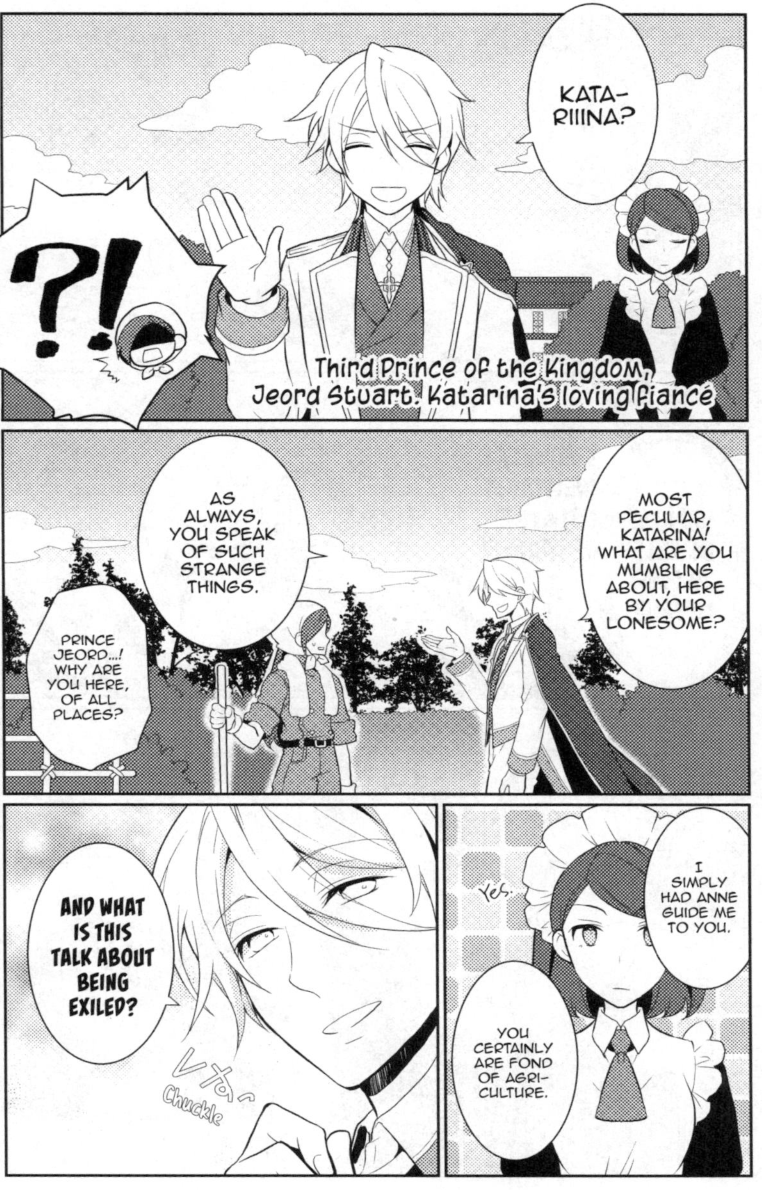
KATA-RIIINA?
?!
Third Prince of the Kingdom, Jeord Stuart. Katarina's loving fiance
MOST PECULIAR, KATARINA! WHAT ARE YOU MUMBLING ABOUT, HERE BY YOUR LONESOME?
AS ALWAYS, YOU SPEAK OF SUCH STRANGE THINGS.
PRINCE JEORD...! WHY ARE YOU HERE, OF ALL PLACES?
I SIMPLY HAD ANNE GUIDE ME TO YOU.
Yes.
YOU CERTAINLY ARE FOND OF AGRI-CULTURE.
AND WHAT IS THIS TALK ABOUT BEING EXILED?
Chuckle

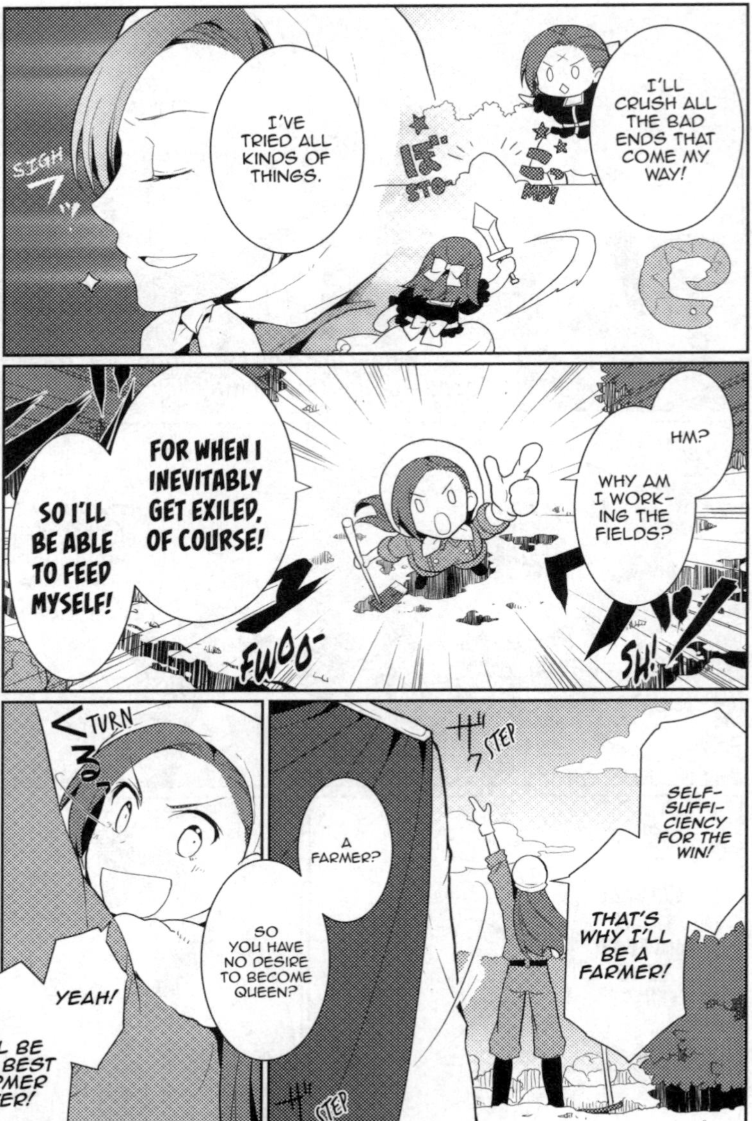
I'LL CRUSH ALL THE BAD ENDS THAT COME MY WAY!
STO-MP!
I'VE TRIED ALL KINDS OF THINGS.
SIGH
HM?
WHY AM I WORKING THE FIELDS?
FOR WHEN I INEVITABLY GET EXILED, OF COURSE!
SO I'LL BE ABLE TO FEED MYSELF!
FWOO-SH!
STEP
SELF-SUFFICIENCY FOR THE WIN!
THAT'S WHY I'LL BE A FARMER!
A FARMER?
SO YOU HAVE NO DESIRE TO BECOME QUEEN?
TURN
YEAH!
I'LL BE THE BEST FARMER EVER!
STEP

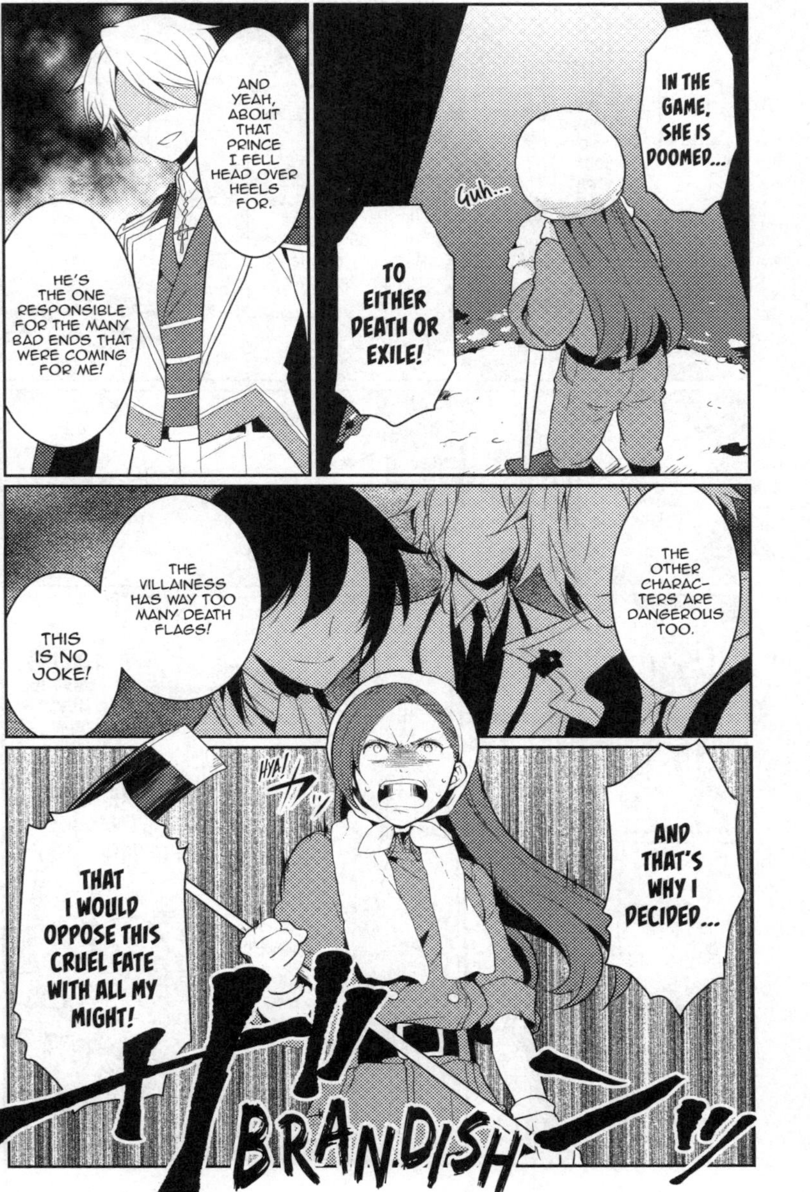

IN THE GAME, SHE IS DOOMED...
Guh...
TO EITHER DEATH OR EXILE!
AND YEAH, ABOUT THAT PRINCE I FELL HEAD OVER HEELS FOR.
HE'S THE ONE RESPONSIBLE FOR THE MANY BAD ENDS THAT WERE COMING FOR ME!
THE OTHER CHARAC-TERS ARE DANGEROUS TOO.
THE VILLAINESS HAS WAY TOO MANY DEATH FLAGS!
THIS IS NO JOKE!
AND THAT'S WHY I DECIDED...
HYA!
THAT I WOULD OPPOSE THIS CRUEL FATE WITH ALL MY MIGHT!
BRANDISH

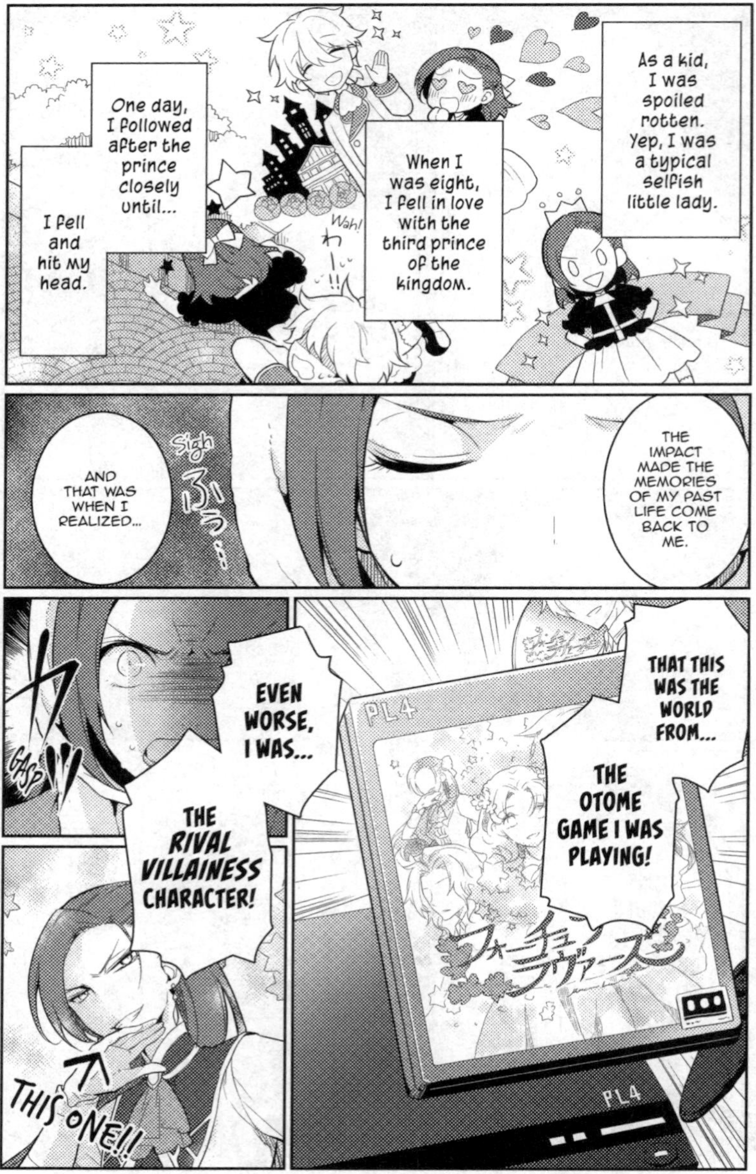

As a kid, I was spoiled rotten. Yep, I was a typical selfish little lady.
When I was eight, I fell in love with the third prince of the kingdom.
Wah!
One day, I followed after the prince closely until...
I fell and hit my head.
THE IMPACT MADE THE MEMORIES OF MY PAST LIFE COME BACK TO ME.
Sigh
AND THAT WAS WHEN I REALIZED...
THAT THIS WAS THE WORLD FROM...
THE OTOME GAME I WAS PLAYING!
PL4
PL4
GASP
EVEN WORSE, I WAS...
THE *RIVAL VILLAINESS* CHARACTER!
THIS ONE!!

SHUK! SHUK! SHUK! SHUK!

While I was a seventeen-year-old high school girl in my past life, I am currently the eldest daughter of Duke Claes.

Hello, I am Katarina Claes.

THONK!

Tiling the soil, of course!

Hm? And what would a noble lady like me be doing?

PHEW

It's a long story, so sit tight.

A lot has happened between then and now.

The Day I Realized I Had Become a Villainess

Contents

J-Novel Club Lineup

Ebook Releases Series List

A Lily Blooms in Another World
A Wild Last Boss Appeared!
Altina the Sword Princess
Amagi Brilliant Park
An Archdemon's Dilemma: How to Love Your Elf Bride
Arifureta Zero
Arifureta: From Commonplace to World's Strongest
Ascendance of a Bookworm
Beatless
Bibliophile Princess
Black Summoner
By the Grace of the Gods
Campfire Cooking in Another World with My Absurd Skill
Can Someone Please Explain What's Going On?!
Cooking with Wild Game
Crest of the Stars
Deathbound Duke's Daughter
Demon Lord, Retry!
Der Werwolf: The Annals of Veight
From Truant to Anime Screenwriter: My Path to "Anohana" and "The Anthem of the Heart"
Full Metal Panic!
Grimgar of Fantasy and Ash
Her Majesty's Swarm
Holmes of Kyoto
How a Realist Hero Rebuilt the Kingdom
How NOT to Summon a Demon Lord
I Refuse to Be Your Enemy!
I Saved Too Many Girls and Caused the Apocalypse
I Shall Survive Using Potions!
In Another World With My Smartphone
Infinite Dendrogram
Infinite Stratos
Invaders of the Rokujouma!?
Isekai Rebuilding Project
JK Haru is a Sex Worker in Another World
Kobold King
Kokoro Connect
Last and First Idol
Lazy Dungeon Master
Mapping: The Trash-Tier Skill That Got Me Into a Top-Tier Party

Middle-Aged Businessman, Arise in Another World!
Mixed Bathing in Another Dimension
Monster Tamer
My Big Sister Lives in a Fantasy World
My Instant Death Ability is So Overpowered, No One in This Other World Stands a Chance Against Me!
My Next Life as a Villainess: All Routes Lead to Doom!
Otherside Picnic
Outbreak Company
Outer Ragna
Record of Wortenia War
Seirei Gensouki: Spirit Chronicles
Sexiled: My Sexist Party Leader Kicked Me Out, So I Teamed Up With a Mythical Sorceress!
Slayers
Sorcerous Stabber Orphen: The Wayward Journey
Tearmoon Empire
Teogonia
The Bloodline
The Combat Butler and Automaton Waitress
The Economics of Prophecy
The Epic Tale of the Reincarnated Prince Herscherik
The Extraordinary, the Ordinary, and SOAP!
The Greatest Magicmaster's Retirement Plan
The Holy Knight's Dark Road
The Magic in this Other World is Too Far Behind!
The Master of Ragnarok & Blesser of Einherjar
The Sorcerer's Receptionist
The Tales of Marielle Clarac
The Underdog of the Eight Greater Tribes
The Unwanted Undead Adventurer
WATARU!! The Hot-Blooded Fighting Teen & His Epic Adventures in a Fantasy World After Stopping a Truck with His Bare Hands!!

The White Cat's Revenge as Plotted from the Demon King's Lap
The World's Least Interesting Master Swordsman
Welcome to Japan, Ms. Elf!
When the Clock Strikes Z
Wild Times with a Fake Fake Princess

Manga Series:
A Very Fairy Apartment
An Archdemon's Dilemma: How to Love Your Elf Bride
Animeta!
Ascendance of a Bookworm
Bibliophile Princess
Black Summoner
Campfire Cooking in Another World with My Absurd Skill
Cooking with Wild Game
Demon Lord, Retry!
Discommunication
How a Realist Hero Rebuilt the Kingdom
I Love Yuri and I Got Bodyswapped with a Fujoshi!
I Shall Survive Using Potions!
Infinite Dendrogram
Mapping: The Trash-Tier Skill That Got Me Into a Top-Tier Party
Marginal Operation
Record of Wortenia War
Seirei Gensouki: Spirit Chronicles
Sorcerous Stabber Orphen: The Reckless Journey
Sorcerous Stabber Orphen: The Youthful Journey
Sweet Reincarnation
The Faraway Paladin
The Magic in this Other World is Too Far Behind!
The Master of Ragnarok & Blesser of Einherjar
The Tales of Marielle Clarac
The Unwanted Undead Adventurer

Keep an eye out at j-novel.club for further new title announcements!

My Next Life as a VILLAINESS: ALL ROUTES LEAD TO DOOM!

VOLUME 5

SATORU YAMAGUCHI
ILLUSTRATIONS BY NAMI HIDAKA

BONUS MANGA SECTION!